Praise for

Abolition and the Underground Railroad in Chester County, Pennsylvania

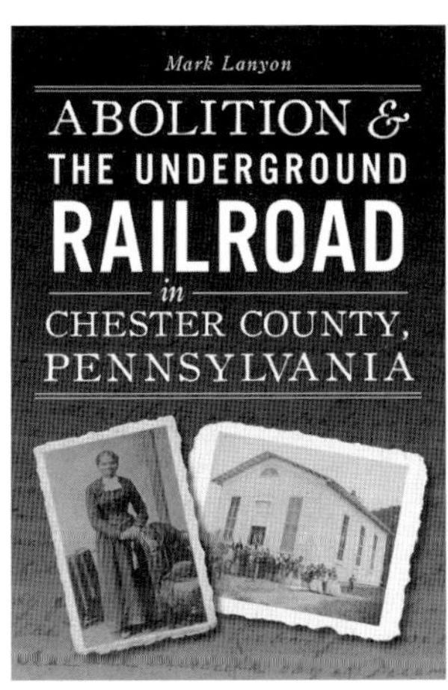

Maya Angelou said that "there is no greater agony than bearing an untold story." Indeed, there is an agony in our nation that the stories, the voices, and the images of slavery, Black Americans, abolition, and the Underground Railroad are so unknown and unseen in our wider understanding of history. This well-researched book gives expressive voice to their subjects and helps to shine fresh light on this agony, and brings to life a more complete picture of the compelling, complex, and heartbreaking and beautiful story that is America.

—Dr. Ernest Levister, whose great-grandfather and great-grand-uncle co-founded Lincoln University with Reverend John Miller Dickey

I am blown away by the history. I had no idea about the Quakers or the immense activity of the Underground Railroad. Rather than lamenting the fact that Lincoln is the only Black college not surrounded by a large African American community, I can now give a better, more inclusive history as one community that supported freedom. And the narrative fits better for the first Black college in the U.S.

—Oliver St. Claire Franklin, CBE,
Honorary British Consul for Greater Philadelphia

LOST
CHESTER COUNTY
PENNSYLVANIA

MARK DEWITT LANYON

Published by The History Press
Charleston, SC
www.historypress.com

Front cover: The Chester County Poorhouse was Pennsylvania's first home for the poverty-stricken. It was a beautiful three-story brick building. *Courtesy of the Chester County History Center.*

Back cover: The Chester County War Aid Association was organized in 1917 to help the soldiers and nurses who were overseas fighting in the war. The CCWAA also provided clothes for those displaced by the war. *Courtesy of the Chester County History Centrer.*

First published 2023

Manufactured in the United States

ISBN 9781467154703

Library of Congress Control Number: 2023940754

Notice: The information in this book is true and complete to the best of our knowledge. It is offered without guarantee on the part of the author or The History Press. The author and The History Press disclaim all liability in connection with the use of this book.

This book is dedicated to the history societies, the history centers, the history associations and their historians (paid and volunteer) who work tirelessly to document, preserve and protect the information about the people, places and events that make up the story of Chester County.

CONTENTS

ACKNOWLEDGEMENTS

I would like to thank the following people for their various roles in helping this book come together:

Alli Davis from the Pennsylvania Historical and Museum Commission.
Sandy Moyer from the Yellow Springs Historical Society.
John Keenan from the Historical Society of the Phoenixville Area.
John "Jack" Ertell from the Historical Society of the Phoenixville Area.
Gail Roberts from the Oxford Area Historical Association.
Sherrill Jones from the New London Area Historical Society.
R. Scott Steele, West Grove Historian.
Judy Ng from the Chester County History Center.
Patrick Bryan, park ranger at the Nottingham Park.
Lorraine Lucas, historian extraordinaire.
Banks Smither from The History Press.
My wife, Beth Ann.

INTRODUCTION

Since retiring, Mark has been able to focus on research about Chester County. His research resulted in his book *Abolition and the Underground Railroad in Chester County, Pennsylvania*. This book covered slavery, the Underground Railroad, the abolitionist movement, the Pennsylvania Yearly Meeting of Progressive Friends (also known as the Longwood Progressive Friends Meeting), Hosanna Church and the founding of Lincoln University.

After Mark's first book came out, people would approach him after his presentations and comment on how they did not know about the Stargazer Stone or the Cox House and the like. That got Mark thinking—what other people, places and events of Chester County do people not know about? And that is how this new book, *Lost Chester County, Pennsylvania*, came into existence.

The book covers the unknown, little-known and forgotten history of Chester County. It is not meant to be an exhaustive exploration of every person, place and event in Chester County. Mark is extremely grateful for the assistance he received from various historical societies, centers and associations. The people at each place were gracious and extremely helpful.

Chapter 1 covers the Native Americans who lived in Chester County. One of the sections covers probably the most famous Leni-Lenape Indian: Indian Hannah.

Chapter 2 explores the fascinating serpentine barrens found in Nottingham Park. This is one of the few places in the world that serpentine barrens are found. So unique and special is this place it was designated a

National Natural Landmark in 2009. There are only 602 such landmarks in the United States.

Chapter 3 looks at villages and buildings that have ceased to exist, have been abandoned or have become new versions of themselves. In this chapter, you will discover how technology and modernization can have their benefits but also their downfalls.

Chapter 4 looks at four different schools. One of the schools produced three signers of the Declaration of Independence. Another cared for orphans whose fathers were killed in the Civil War. Another school was named after quartz stones, which are as hard as diamonds and can cut glass.

Chapter 5 looks at the role of manufacturing in Chester County. At one time, Chester County was home to a highly successful caramel factory. One manufacturing plant produced a cannon that tipped the scales in favor of the Union army in the Civil War. At one point, there was a spring water bottling plant. Although all that remains of the plant is stone ruins, the springs are still active.

Chapter 6 looks at entertainment and recreation in Chester County. One place was home to country and bluegrass music north of the Mason-Dixon line.

Chapter 7 explores the Underground Railroad and the abolitionist movement in Chester County. Because of the work of one group of people, President Lincoln wrote, presented to Congress and eventually signed the Emancipation Proclamation.

Chapter 8 presents the work Chester County women did to bring about the right for women to vote.

Chapter 9 covers wartime in Chester County, ranging from the Revolutionary War to the Vietnam War. It also highlights the man who discovered how to mass-produce penicillin, thereby saving numerous lives.

Chapter 1

NATIVE AMERICANS IN CHESTER COUNTY

CHESTER COUNTY: THE LENI-LENAPES

The Leni-Lenapes consisted of three tribes: the Minsis or Munsees, known as "People of the Stone Country"; the Unamis, known as "People Who Live Down River"; and the Unalachtigos, known as "People Who Live by the Ocean." The Unamis were the ones who lived in Chester County.

There were no large communities of Lenapes. Instead, they would usually live in small camps of twenty to thirty people. Their houses consisted of wigwams that had no windows but did have an opening at the top to allow smoke to exit the dwelling.

The Minguannan Indian Town was one of the largest camps, numbering about 200 people. There was a total of about 1,200 Leni-Lenapes in the area. The Leni-Lenapes were known as the "common or original people." The Lenapes in this area spoke Unami, which was the language of the Algonquin Indians.

The Leni-Lenapes named the major river near them the Lenapewihittuk, or River of the Lenape. The European settlers renamed the river the Delaware River after Thomas West, the 3rd Baron De La Warr. That is the reason European settlers often referred to the Leni-Lenapes as the Delaware Indians.

During the summer months, the women would grow and harvest what was known as the "three sisters": beans, squash and corn. The men would hunt small game and fish. During the winter months, the Lenapes would travel to camps farther north, where men would hunt large game, including deer and bear. Women would teach the girls how to gather plants, seeds, nuts and clams, as well as how to tan hides and make clothing. The men would teach the boys how to hunt for wild game. Leni-Lenapes did not have long life expectancies. Because of this, both the men and women married in their early teen years. As happens in all societies, some marriages lasted while others ended in divorce. When a Lenape wife wanted a divorce, she would put all her husband's belongings outside the wigwam. If the husband wanted a divorce, he would simply leave.

Prior to William Penn coming to establish Pennsylvania, he had never encountered an Indian. On the other hand, the Leni-Lenapes of Chester County had met with Dutch traders, who offered alcohol, textiles and tools in exchange for furs. Once it was realized what price the furs could fetch in Europe, other traders came to the area, including the Swedes and Finns.

As more settlers arrived from Europe, many Lenapes, including the Okehockings, decided it was time to move west. The Okehockings finally settled in Oklahoma. Some of the Lenapes moved eastward into what is now New Jersey in order to escape from their mortal enemy, the Minquas (also known as Susquehannocks). Not all Lenapes migrated to the west, and some live in the tri-state area of Pennsylvania, New Jersey and Delaware. Each year, the Nanticoke-Lenape Indians hold a powwow in Woodstown, New Jersey, that is open to the public. There are two other Nanticoke-Lenape gatherings held in south Jersey that the public cannot attend.

Although Pennsylvania was once the center of Lenape life, it is one of the few states that does not have a reservation nor acknowledges any native tribe. There are no Pennsylvania college and/or university courses focusing on Native American studies. The Pennsylvania Department of Education mandates that students learn about Native Americans. Sadly, a review of ten different middle school and high school textbooks revealed that there was only one sentence about the Lenape Indians in the textbooks.

KENNETT SQUARE: INDIAN HANNAH

There is one name that is synonymous with the Leni-Lenapes: Hannah Freeman, better known as Indian Hannah. Born to Lenape parents in about 1730, Hannah Freeman lived with her parents on the property owned by Quaker William Webb. Hannah's family consisted of "a grandmother, two aunts, and two brothers."

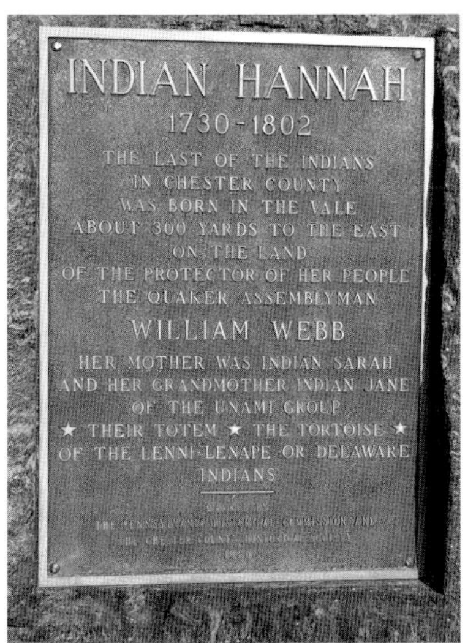

Indian Hannah was born and grew up in a cabin near what is now Longwood Gardens. *Courtesy of the Pennsylvania Historical and Museum Commission.*

During the winter months, Hannah's family lived in cabins on the Webb property, and during the summer months, they migrated to camps close to the Brandywine River so they could fish and plant corn. Hannah and her family experienced what so many other Lenapes did, the encroachment on their summer camps. Hannah's father, along with others, made the decision to move west from the Brandywine Valley to the Susquehanna Valley.

After hearing about the massacre of the Indians of Conestoga Indian Town led by the Paxton Boys in December 1763, Hannah's father once again moved the family—this time across the Delaware River into New Jersey. Seven years later, Hannah moved back to Chester County.

Hannah never married and had a small farm where she grew the three sisters. Along with raising cows and pigs, she also fished. Hannah's income came from her ability as a basket weaver and maker of brooms. She was also known to work on nearby Quaker farms. In later life, when she could no longer maintain her farm, she worked for her room and board by living with various Quaker households in Chester County. As her health declined and her ability to work for room and board lessened, the Quaker community came to view Hannah as a charity case.

In 1797, Indian Hannah was "legally declared indigent," and on November 12, 1800, she became one of the first residents of the newly opened Chester County Poorhouse. Two years later, Hannah died and was buried on the property. Indian Hannah was a poor working woman. Once asked what her adult life was like, she responded that she considered herself "a migrant domestic worker."

Many Lenapes migrated westward to escape the vast numbers of European settlers encroaching on their lands. However, others chose to stay and become part of the fast-changing culture. Today, some live in the tri-state area of Pennsylvania, New Jersey and Delaware.

Historically, Indian Hannah is often referred to as the last Leni-Lenape living in Chester County, which is not accurate. The Quakers apparently

Above: The marker for the cabin Indian Hannah grew up in is located on the grounds of the Longwood Progressive Friends Meetinghouse. *Author's collection.*

Opposite: Indian Hannah Cross, located within the grounds of Longwood Gardens. *Author's collection.*

were aware that Hannah Freeman was not the last and that there were other Lenapes living in Chester County.

So, why was Indian Hannah declared the last surviving Lenape in Chester County? One theory is apparently that Hannah's Quaker neighbors were living on land that had never been sold or given to them by the Lenapes. However, the declaration of Hannah being the last surviving Lenape fulfilled William Penn's pledge that Lenape land that had not been sold to or given to settlers rightfully belonged to the Lenapes until the land was abandoned by either moving west or by death.

William Penn stipulated in all his treaties with the Lenapes that "unoccupied" Lenape land could be sold. Exactly what constituted "unoccupied" was never clarified. The nomadic Lenapes would move winter and summer to fish and hunt. It was not uncommon to return from their winters in the north to their fishing camps in the south only to discover that these camps had been declared "unoccupied" and sold to willing settlers.

Although Indian Hannah cannot be remembered as being the last of the Leni-Lenapes in Chester County, she can be remembered for being the embodiment of the Lenape nomad who migrated winter and summer and followed the hunting, fishing and growing seasons. Indian Hannah also represented what it looked like for European settlers and the Lenapes to grow and learn from one another.

Chester County wanted to honor Indian Hannah, so in 1925 the Pennsylvania Historical Commission and the Chester County Historical Society agreed to have a historical marker created. By now the Webb property was part of Longwood Gardens, so owner Pierre duPont donated land on which the marker was to be placed.

In response to numerous traffic accidents, Longwood Gardens agreed to have a portion of Route 52 relocated. The project was completed in 2012. The historic marker honoring Indian Hannah was no longer accessible to the general public, and Longwood Gardens officials agreed that the monument should be relocated.

On May 15, 2014, the historic marker was moved to its new location on the property of the Longwood Progressive Friends Meetinghouse, which is owned by Longwood Gardens.

Within Longwood Gardens there is still a marker to memorialize Indian Hannah. You walk through the Peirce Woods, and instead of going downhill toward the Italian Fountains, you turn left, reach a "T" junction and turn right. There you will find a small sign. Looking into the woods, you will see a memorial cross.

During Victorian times, it was common to have a memorial grave and marker and/or headstone to honor someone. George Washington Peirce, the great-great-grandson of the first owner of the property that would become Longwood Gardens, began this tradition of honoring Indian Hannah. When Pierre S. duPont purchased the property, he continued the tradition by having the memorial grave and cross maintained. Today, the staff of Longwood Gardens continues this tradition.

WILLISTOWN TOWNSHIP: OKEHOCKING PRESERVE

The Okehocking tribe were part of the Leni-Lenapes. The Okehockings spoke Unami and were part of the Unamis, which was one of the three Leni-Lenape geographic groups. Unami means "people down the river." Native Americans identified various tribes according to where they lived.

Upon arriving in the colonies, William Penn made it clear that settlers were not allowed to seize land that belonged to the Native Americans. Only if the Lenapes sold or signed over land could settlers build and live on that Lenape land. However, the Okehockings, worried that they would be removed from their lands as colonists further encroached on native lands, met with the William Penn and the Provincial Council in 1701. A request made for permanent land was granted, so they would no longer have to fear being removed from their land. William Penn sold them five hundred acres of land.

The request was granted to the Unami tribe, whose symbol was the tortoise. The Unamis believed that the tortoise portrayed the earth and that the tortoise acted as an "intermediary between the visible and the invisible worlds around them." On the land that ultimately became the Okehocking Indian Town, there is a rock outcropping that looks like a turtle head. Most likely this is the reason they chose that particular grant of five hundred acres in October 1702.

The Willistown location became the summer home of the Okehocking clan until about 1735. The main crop raised during the summer months was maize. The women gathered fruits and nuts, and the men provided small game and fish. During the winter months, they migrated to the upper Schuylkill area, where the men spent their time hunting large game. Prior to the settlers purchasing land and setting up farms with defined borders, the Okehockings traveled wherever they chose in order to hunt game; property lines did not mean anything to them.

Until the Penn Grant, there were no defined property lines for the Indian villages. In order to avoid legal issues, settlers would build their homes away from Indian camps. Once the Penn Grant was approved and the Okehockings had defined property lines, settlers felt comfortable building settlements up to and around the property lines without breaking the law. Ironically, what began as a way to prevent settlers from encroaching on their property resulted in settlers living too close to the tribe.

Because of this, the Okehocking began to consider moving, and around 1735 they moved west. Ultimately, they made Oklahoma their home. Some chose farming as a profession, and others became shopkeepers. The

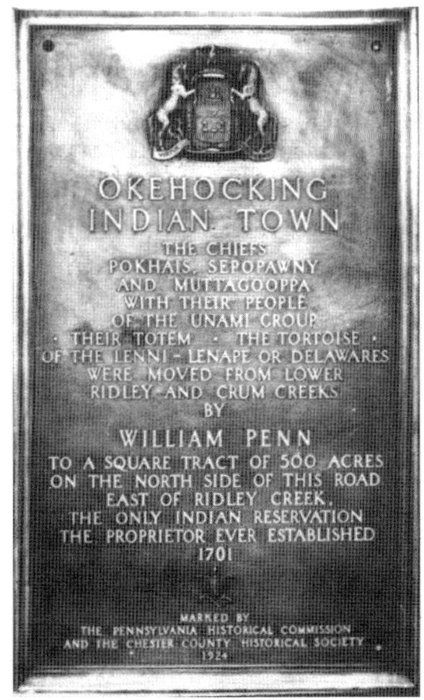

Left: Close-up of the plaque on a marker for the Okehocking Town, which came about when William Penn sold the Okehockings' five hundred acres of land. *Author's collection.*

Right: Sign for the Okehocking Preserve. *Author's collection.*

Okehocking Indian Town, having been considered abandoned, was taken over in 1738 by the Yarnall brothers, James and Mordecai.

The site of the former Okehocking Indian Town is located in Willistown Township, Chester County. A Pennsylvania Historic and Museum Commission historical marker was dedicated on June 21, 1924. There is a large boulder to which is mounted a bronze marker, which notes that the former Okehocking Indian Town is "the only Indian Reservation the Proprietor [William Penn] ever established."

Known as the Okehocking Preserve, it consists of 155 acres of the original 500-acre land grant given by William Penn. There are trails through the preserve. The address for the preserve is 5316 West Chester Pike, Newtown Square, Pennsylvania.

LANDENBERG: MINGUANNAN INDIAN TOWN

One of the largest Indian towns in Chester County was the Minguannan Indian Town. The town was located on the banks of the White Clay Creek. It is estimated that two hundred Lenapes lived there. The White Clay Creek Preserve consists of land that belonged to the Lenapes. In 1683, the land was sold by Lenape chief Kekelappen to William Penn. Evidence uncovered by archaeologists suggests that the Lenapes of Minguannan lived there from the Archaic Period until it was sold in 1683, for a total of nearly eight thousand years.

The Lenape women here cultivated the three sisters. Their homes were one-room wigwams. Living up to the current name of White Clay Creek Preserve, the Lenapes used white clay from the creek beds to form pottery. Housewares were made from local red clay.

John Evans, a Welsh Baptist, came to the colony of Pennsylvania to escape religious persecution and begin a new life. In 1714, he met with William Penn and purchased four hundred acres. This was land that William Penn had purchased from Chief Kekelappen.

John Evans was instrumental in the building of the London Tract Baptist Meetinghouse. In 1725, Evans donated the land he had purchased along with the meetinghouse to the new congregation. In spite of the large Quaker presence in Chester County, it was actually the Welsh Baptists who first settled in the White Clay Creek Preserve area.

The London Tract Meetinghouse still stands today, and there are informative lectures given throughout the year. The cemetery has graves of

Above: In front of the London Tract Friends Meetinghouse, there is a marker indicating the site of the Minguannan Indian Town. *Author's collection.*

Left: Close-up of the plaque on the marker in front of the London Tract Friends Meetinghouse. *Author's collection.*

people who were born in England. The grave of John Evans is located in the cemetery. Perhaps the most famous grave is the "Ticking Tomb."

Legend has it that in 1763, Jeremiah Dixon and Charles Mason were working nearby. Along with surveying for the Mason-Dixon boundary line, Charles was trying to create a watch that would tell better time than the one he currently had. Supposedly, a young boy was looking around the camp and, accidentally or not, swallowed the watch Mason was working on. Ironically, the young boy grew up and repaired clocks for a profession. He is buried at the London Tract Meetinghouse graveyard. People claim that you can still hear the watch inside him ticking away.

Today, there is a historic marker acknowledging the town. The plaque is mounted to a boulder that sits in front of the London Tract Meetinghouse. The marker was placed by the Pennsylvania Historical Commission and the Chester County Historical Society in 1926.

WEST CHESTER: GREAT MINQUAS PATH

Prior to European fur traders arriving, the Native Americans had a highly efficient, well-developed system of paths on which to travel. Rather than building their own paths, the Europeans utilized the ones already in existence.

The Susquehannocks and Lenapes used these paths as they migrated from summer fishing camps to winter hunting camps. They were also used during wartime. The Susquehannocks arrived on the Great Minquas Path to attack the Lenapes. That is why the Lenapes named the Susquehannocks "Minqua," which meant "treacherous." The Dutch were the ones who named the fur trading trail the "Great Minquas Trail" after the Minqua Indians.

The Great Minquas Path was a trade route that ran for about eighty miles between two major rivers: the Susquehanna and the Schuylkill. The Great Minquas Trail of the Leni-Lenapes connected the lower Schuylkill Valley trading posts with the areas where the beaver pelts were found. This was the main trading route for the Susquehannocks, who traded furs with the Dutch, English and Swedes. The Dutch were the first to trade with the Susquehannocks, which began in the 1620s. The Dutch named the trail "Beversreede," which translated means Beaver Road—an appropriate name for those trading in beaver pelts.

The Dutch, in the 1620s, were the first Europeans to enter the fur trade. The Dutch built Fort Beversreede around 1633. Around 1638, the Swedes

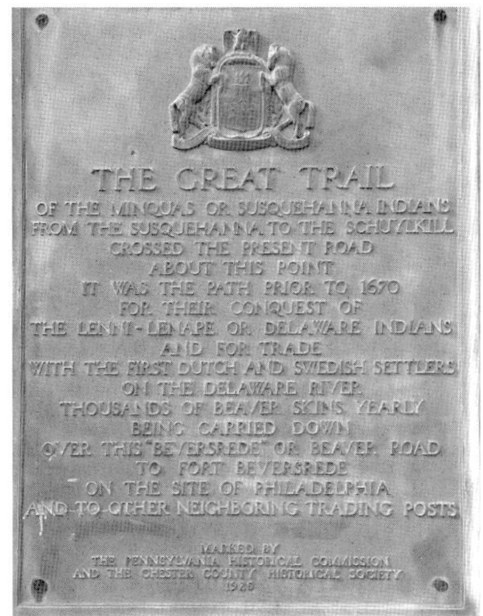

Left: The Great Minquas was a trade route that the Dutch named "Beversreede," which translated means Beaver Road. Many beaver pelts were carried along this trade route. *Courtesy of the Pennsylvania Historical and Museum Commission.*

Right: Close-up of the plaque for the Great Minquas Path. *Courtesy of the Pennsylvania Historical and Museum Commision.*

entered the fur trade and established a Swedish colony named New Sweden, which was about twenty miles south of Fort Beversreede.

Realizing how profitable the fur trade was, the Swedes unsuccessfully tried to gain control over the fur trade from the Dutch. When that attempt did not work, the Swedes blockaded Fort Beversreede. The Dutch, finding the fort no longer useful, abandoned it in 1651. Four years later, the Dutch came back, defeated the Swedes and gave New Sweden the new name of New Amsterdam. The English had their turn, and in 1664, they defeated the Dutch.

Today, Strasburg Road in Chester County for the most part follows what was then the Great Minquas Path. Travelers going between Philadelphia and Lancaster have two main routes to use: Route 30 and the Pennsylvania Turnpike. In so doing, one is roughly following the Great Minquas Path. This path played a major role as the fledgling economy grew.

The Great Minquas Path helped create immense wealth for the European fur traders. Over time, the path went from a well-used footpath to a highway that stills carry valuable commerce to consumers.

NEWLIN TOWNSHIP: RETURN OF THE LENI-LENAPE BURIAL GROUND

Located on a hill overlooking the west branch of the Brandywine Creek near Northbrook, Pennsylvania, there is a Lenape burial ground. Due to the nomadic nature of the Lenapes, this is the only documented Lenape burial ground in Chester County.

The Lenape burial ceremony was not complicated. After a shallow grave was dug, one of two ways for the burial of body was followed. One way was to line the grave with tree bark, dried plants or grass. The other way was to first place the body in a coffin. Various items might be placed on and/or with the corpse. This could include necklaces of beads received through fur trading. After the body or the coffin was placed in the ground, it was then covered with soil followed by bark and leaves. By having no fresh ground exposed, this reduced the likelihood of animals being alerted to the presence of the body and digging it up.

The Lenapes believed that when one of their people died, the spirt and the body separated. Believing that the spirit remained at the community for eleven days, Lenapes would leave food offerings at the grave site for the spirit to receive nourishment prior to traveling at the end of the eleven days to the Creator or Great Spirit.

After a Lenape died, his or her name was never spoken again. To do so would cause great sadness for the family. The Lenapes believed that there were two deaths that occurred when one of their people died: the person and the person's name.

Indian Knoll Farm is located near the Brandywine River. On the property is an Indian burial ground that was donated to the ancestors of the Leni-Lenape Indians. *Author's collection.*

The land where the burial ground is located was once owned by Caleb Marshall. He had noticed that there were at least thirty indentations in the ground, which indicated burial sites. Having heard about the burial ground, the Philosophical Society of West Chester in 1878 reached out to Mr. Marshall to request and receive permission to examine the graves.

In 1878, members of the Philosophical Society came out to the burial site, located six miles from West Chester and one mile from Northbrook. Four graves were uncovered by

H. Rush Kervey. The first grave exhumed revealed a skeleton on its back at a depth of about three feet. The skeleton was facing from east to west, and the head was placed such that the face "looked" northwest. A necklace made of nineteen Venetian beads was found around the neck of the skeleton. The beads indicated that the Lenapes had been trading with the Europeans.

The second grave yielded a skeleton with its face turned upward. There was a necklace consisting of amber-colored European beads and blue and white Venetian beads. Also found were two gun-flints, which apparently had been handcrafted by the Lenapes. Surrounding the skeleton were a number of wrought-iron nails that had pieces of wood attached to them. This seemed to indicate that the Lenapes had been buried in a coffin, which was in keeping with the Lenape tradition. The third grave yielded a skull and some decomposed bones. Other than one coffin nail, there were no other items found. The fourth grave only contained some fragments of bones.

In 1899, two Swarthmore professors, Spencer Trotter and Bird Baldwin, exhumed another grave. They found a skeleton six feet, one inch tall lying on a floor made of stone. The skeleton was facing east. Accompanying the skeleton were glass beads and objects made of copper. On February 20, 1908, Professor Baldwin provided a report of their findings to the Chester County Historical Society. The next year, the historical society erected a marker.

In 1987, Carol McCloskey purchased 170 acres known as Indian Knoll Farm. The property was subdivided, and 10-acre plots were sold. However, the half-acre burial ground was deeded, stating that it had to remain intact in perpetuity.

In 2021, Mrs. McCloskey wanted to donate the burial ground to Native Americans. Her attorney utilized the Native American Graves Protection and Repatriation Act, which allows burial sites to be "transferred to culturally affiliated tribes." With that in mind, there was a search for any group that might be affiliated with the Lenapes who were buried there.

Her lawyer located a group to whom the burial ground could be transferred: the Delaware Nation, located in Anadarko, Oklahoma. The ancestors of the Delaware Nation were Lenapes from Chester County who had migrated westward to escape the continued encroachment by the European settlers. Carol McCloskey sold the half-acre burial ground to the Delaware Nation in February 2022 for the sum of one dollar.

The transaction was recorded at the Prothonotary's Office at the West Chester Court House, and this piece of history has been returned to its rightful owners and is forever protected.

Chapter 2

NOTTINGHAM PARK SERPENTINE BARRENS

NOTTINGHAM: SERPENTINE BARRENS

Located in the southeastern corner of Chester County is a favorite and tasty tourist site: the Herrs Snack Factory. Driving along the entranceway to the factory, you come to a crossroad. To the left is the visitor parking lot, straight ahead the employee parking lot and to the right is Park Road. Driving a mile and half on Park Road takes you to the Nottingham County Park.

This park is a favorite spot for picnics, wedding receptions and baseball games. There is also a fishing lake and a riding ring and trails for those equestrians who wish to bring their own horses. Nottingham Park, opened in 1963, is Chester County's first county park.

Unbeknownst to many coming to this park, this area is one of three locations in North American where serpentine stone can be found. The Nottingham Park Serpentine Barrens consists of a deposit of serpentine rock more than one square mile in diameter. Serpentine was discovered here in 1828. The Wood Mine quarried serpentine (along with chromite, asbestos and quartz), and by 1880, it had reached a depth of eight hundred feet, which was the largest in the world at that time. As a testament to mining operations located at the park in the past, there are abandoned serpentine and feldspar quarries along with former chromite mines.

So, just what is serpentine? According to the dictionary, it is "a mineral or rock consisting chiefly of the hydrous silicate of magnesia. It is usually of an obscure green color, often with a spotted or mottled appearance resembling a serpent." Serpentine formed beneath the ocean. During the formation of

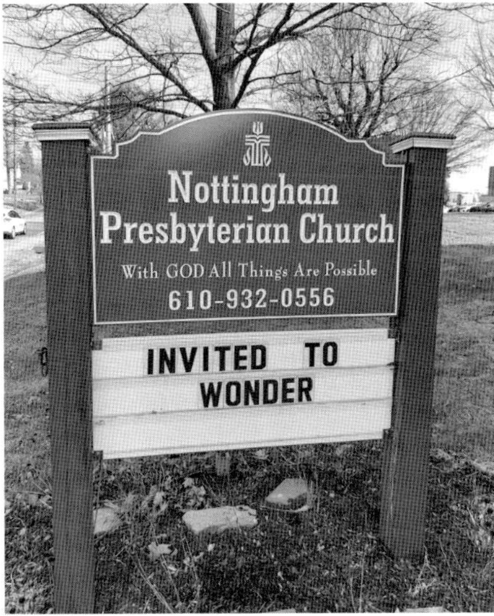

Above, left: Nottingham Park offers many recreational activities but is also home to the Nottingham Park Serpentine Barrens. *Author's collection.*

Above, right: The Nottingham Church was built of serpentine stone mined from the Nottingham Park Serpentine Barrens. *Author's collection.*

Left: The Nottingham Church is located less than five miles from the serpentine barrens—one reason the church utilized a readily available building material. *Author's collection.*

The serpentine barrens are so named due to the high levels of toxic metals, which limit what vegetation can grow on the soil. *Author's collection.*

the earth's continents, some of the serpentine was pushed upward, being deposited on only a few sites in the world.

As you drive around Chester County, you will see many older buildings made from this light-green rock. The Nottingham Presbyterian Church, close to the Herrs Snack Factory, is made of serpentine extracted from the Dunlap and Martin Quarry in 1878.

The shallow topsoil that makes up the serpentine barrens lacks many of the essential nutrients plants need to thrive. Furthermore, the soil also contains high levels of toxic metals such as nickel and chromium. The shallow soil and the rock it sits on are unable to hold water, resulting in a dry landscape. Because of these three factors, most plants cannot grow here. The term *barrens* was used by early farmers to describe the soil—it was "barren," unable to produce crops due to its poor condition. Indeed, most crops could not grow here.

Because of the limited vegetation that can grow on the barrens, the landscape is similar to the prairies of the U.S. Midwest and the savannahs of Africa. There is grassland punctuated with an occasional scrub pine tree. Farmers would utilize the barrens to set out their livestock, primarily sheep, to graze on the grasslands.

Once the serpentine barrens were determined to be of little use for raising crops, the farmers realized that the light green stone could be quarried for use as a distinctive building material. Many buildings in Chester County were built with this beautiful stone.

Serpentine is no longer used as a building material because it does not hold up well to elements, including acid rain. Furthermore, it was discovered that when serpentine was cut into building blocks, asbestos was exposed. The serpentine operations of the Dunlap and Martin Quarry have ceased, and serpentine is no longer extracted from the barrens. However, the Nottingham County Park is still open and offers visitors a chance to tour just what makes the serpentine barrens such a unique and special place.

NOTTINGHAM: CHROMITE

Some visitors coming to the Nottingham County Park are aware of the extensive history of mining that took place there. The serpentine barrens were home to serpentine and feldspar quarries along with chromite ore mines. Before 1865, all the chromite ore produced in the United States came from the serpentine barrens. By 1850, the serpentine barrens of Nottingham

Water-filled chromite mine located within the Nottingham Park Serpentine Barrens. By 1850, the serpentine barrens of Nottingham had become the largest source of chromite in the world. *Author's collection.*

had become the largest source of chromite in the world, and Isaac Tyson Jr. held a monopoly over the world's supply of chromite.

There were two major chromite ore mines in the barrens: the Scott Mine and the Engine Mine. The Scott Mine, owned by the Tyson Mining Company, produced between three thousand and six thousand tons of chromite and reached a depth of between two hundred and four hundred feet.

Two events occurred in the 1820s that influenced the world. The first was Isaac Tyson's growing monopoly over chromite ore. The second was Andreas Kurtz moving to England.

Isaac Tyson Jr. studied chemistry in France, which helped him understand that serpentine and chromite went hand in hand. Armed with this knowledge, Tyson purchased the serpentine barrens in Nottingham among others. By the 1820s, Tyson had created a chromite monopoly by owning the largest deposits of chromite in the world. For the next twenty years, Tyson was the major supplier of chromite in the world.

The Nottingham chromite ore, mined by Tyson, was sent to Philadelphia, where it used to manufacture paint pigment. At the time, this was the only plant of its kind in the United States. The Nottingham chromite ore was also shipped to Liverpool, England, where it was used in the textile industry.

Prior to synthetic dyes, there were only natural dyes. The problem was that clothes colored with natural dyes faded quickly when laundered. The textile manufacturers in England discovered that chromium, when combined with natural dyes, produced a dyed textile that did not fade as much. Tyson's exporting of chromite to Philadelphia and Liverpool, while holding a monopoly over the chromite industry, made him the "Chrome King of the World."

Andreas Kurtz moved to England in 1822 and began selling chromium to the English textile industry. When competitors started doing likewise, the profit margin dropped significantly. Kurtz then began producing chrome pigments, one of which was his "chrome yellow" pigment.

Princess Charlotte, daughter of King George IV, liked Kurtz's chrome yellow pigment and had all her carriages painted that color, and soon her bright-yellow carriages could be seen throughout the city. Thus was the inspiration for the yellow taxi cabs driving around New York City, as well as the yellow school buses seen throughout the United States. The iconic yellow is known as "Kurtz yellow" and is still available as a paint in England.

The chromite ore mines at Nottingham continued to produce large amounts of chromite for the world's consumption. Then, in the late 1800s, chromite deposits were discovered in South Africa and Rhodesia that were larger than the ones at Nottingham, resulting in a lower demand for the Nottingham chromite. Because of the larger deposits of chromite in South Africa and Rhodesia, local mining of chromite became cost prohibitive and the mines of Nottingham closed.

NOTTINGHAM: FELDSPAR

The nonmetallic mineral feldspar was mined at the Nottingham Serpentine Barrens from 1897 until the early 1900s. At the height of feldspar mining, southeastern Pennsylvania, including the barrens, was one of three largest feldspar producers in the United States.

The main feldspar quarry in the serpentine barrens was called the Brandywine Quarry. This quarry earned the nickname the "Mystery Hole"; it was two hundred feet long, seventy-five feet wide and close to one hundred feet deep. This quarry was a significant producer of feldspar up until the early 1900s.

There was a wave of immigration during the late 1800s and early 1900s. The Brandywine Quarry employed twenty immigrants from the town of Fera San Martino in Abruzzo, Italy. These immigrants worked twelve-hour days and earned $1.25 daily. Steam powered the equipment that was used in this quarry—steam for the derrick, which removed the feldspar; steam for the pump to keep water out of the quarry; and steam for the steam drills, which the laborers used to loosen and remove the feldspar.

The quarried feldspar was sent to two locations. Sparvetta Mining Company purchased some of the output, which was shipped to its factory, where it was ground to be used in ceramics. The other output was shipped to the Brandywine Summit Kaolin and Feldspar Company. After being ground and processed, the feldspar powder was used in a variety of products, including false teeth, porcelain and ceramics.

The Brandywine Feldspar Quarry got the nickname the "Mystery Hole" due to rumors of what might be at the bottom of the quarry. Workers had dug a twenty-foot-square hole at the bottom of the quarry and had dug down approximately twenty feet when they uncovered a spring. The water filled the hole, and the pumps could not keep up with the water flow. The quarry was abandoned at that point.

In 1963, members of the Southern Chester County Scuba Club were practicing in the Brandywine Quarry when they discovered an old automobile. It was a 1929 Graham Paige roadster, under sixty feet of water. How it got there nobody knows.

The water-filled feldspar quarry located in the serpentine barrens was nicknamed the "Mystery Hole" because a variety of things were discovered in the water, including a 1929 Graham Paige roadster car. *Author's collection.*

NOTTINGHAM: NATIONAL NATURAL LANDMARK

The Nottingham Serpentine Barrens is home to one of Pennsylvania's most unusual landscapes. The shallow topsoil sitting on the serpentine does not contain a very high percentage of essential nutrients. What is found in serpentine barrens is a high level of chromium, nickel and magnesium, all of which will kill most plants. Furthermore, the serpentine rock near the surface lead to high temperatures in the soil. All these factors have resulted in unique and rare species of plants, including the serpentine aster and the round-leafed fameflower.

The serpentine aster is found only at the Nottingham Serpentine Barrens and on the serpentine barrens in Maryland and nowhere else in the world. The fameflower is a succulent that stores water in its leaves much like a cactus would do. The barrens chickweed is found at Nottingham and one other location in Chester County and nowhere else in the world. The chickweed has hairy leaves that act as insulation from the heat and sunlight.

Native bobcats live in the serpentine barrens. There are insects located within the barrens that are found nowhere else on the East Coast. There is also the resident of warmer climates, the smooth green snake, that enjoys the warm serpentine rock topsoil. All together there's a dozen plant and animal species that have been designated rare and endangered.

The National Natural Landmark Program was begun in order to preserve places throughout the United States that had unique biological and geological aspects. A National Natural Landmark evaluation was done to consider "whether the resources at Nottingham Park Serpentine Barrens are intact, nationally significant, and deserving of a National Natural Landmark designation." The evaluation of the Nottingham Park Serpentine Barrens was completed and a report submitted on January 18, 2007.

The evaluation found that the Nottingham Potential National Natural Landmark (PNNL) "meets the national significance criteria required for the NNL Program. The proposed site supports shallow serpentine rock outcrops and unique vegetation communities, especially serpentine grassland and open savanna communities. Historic mine sites provide glimpses of the underlying geology, illustrate the history of human use of the area and also serve as good habitat for rare species….After considerable research, discourse with experts, and site visits we have come to the conclusion that Nottingham PNNL contains the required biological and geological features to be listed as a National Natural Landmark," according to Todd Lookingbill's *Evaluation of the Nottingham Park Serpentine Barrens, Chester County, Pennsylvania*.

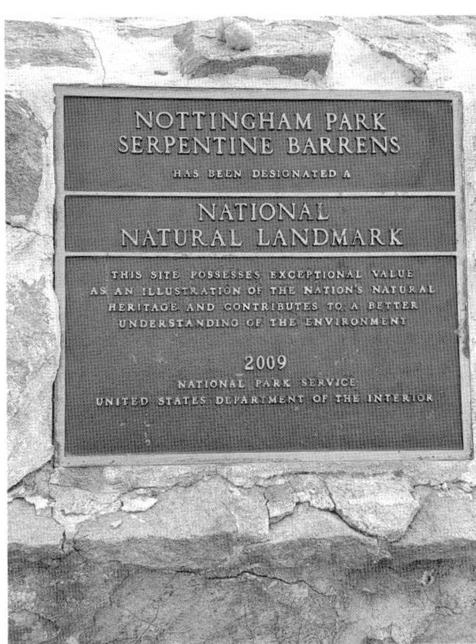

Left: The National Park Service declared the Nottingham Park Serpentine Barrens an official National Natural Landmark in 2009. The marker is located within the park. *Author's collection.*

Right: Close-up of the plaque on the National Natural Landmark marker. *Author's collection.*

The evaluation was completed on January 18, 2007, and the National Park Service declared the Nottingham Park Serpentine Barrens an official National Natural Landmark in 2009. There are only 602 designated National Natural Landmarks in the United States. The Nottingham Park Serpentine Barrens National Natural Landmark is located completely within Nottingham Park.

The serpentine and feldspar quarries and the chromite mines are no longer operational. However, you can hike the trails at Nottingham Park and view the feldspar quarry and the chromite mine sites. You can also hike along the serpentine barrens and see the unusual and rare plant life that exists there and hardly anywhere else in the world.

The address for Nottingham Park is 150 Park Road Nottingham, Pennsylvania, 19362. The park is open daily from 8:00 a.m. until sunset but is closed on Christmas Day.

Chapter 3

VILLAGES/BUILDINGS

EAST COVENTRY TOWNSHIP: FRICK'S LOCKS VILLAGE

Long before European settlers walked the land that comprised Frick's Lock Village, the Lenapes lived on the land. Living next to the Schuylkill River provided the Lenapes the opportunity to trap beaver for their pelts. Along with beaver, the Schuylkill River was a ready source of fish.

In 1681, change began to take place with this land. King Charles II owed William Penn's father, Sir William, money. In order to resolve the debt, the king gave a large portion of land that would eventually become the Commonwealth of Pennsylvania. What was to become Frick's Lock Village began with land grants and purchases made in 1749 and 1764.

John Frick and Catherine Grumbacher were married in 1781. They moved on to the Grumbacher farm, which included a 1757 farmhouse believed to be the first building of the Frick's Lock Village. John Frick's wife died, and John inherited all the land which would become Frick's Lock Village.

The village became an important part of the Schuylkill Canal, which was chartered in 1815. When the canal was completed, part of the canal ran through the village with a double lock being close to the 1757 farmhouse. The Schuylkill Navigation Company built Locks no. 54 and no. 55 on land purchased from John Frick. The sleepy farming community took on the name Frick's Locks after John Frick and the locks that were built on land purchased from him.

With commerce moving up and down the canal, the village grew and became prosperous. The boatmen needed a place to stop, eat and buy supplies. Passengers needed to obtain dinner, and if going inland on a stagecoach, they spent the night in the village.

Commerce along the canal continued to increase, and in 1832, the canal was improved in order to have larger boats navigate the canal. This allowed more coal to be available to businesses located along the canal. With increased canal traffic came an increase in business for the people of Frick's Lock.

As Frick's Locks Village grew, the railroad took notice, and the Frick's Locks station was built in the 1880s. The Pennsylvania Schuylkill Valley Railroad at that time named the station Frick's Lock. As a testament to the continued growth of the village, a U.S. Post Office was opened in the 1890s.

Even though the canal had been improved, new and more efficient modes of transportation developed. As the railroads grew and roads were improved so trucks could more easily deliver commerce, the canal traffic diminished and the Schuylkill Canal business slowed down in the mid-1920s and continued until 1931. The canal was completely filled in by the 1950s. Without the business generated by the canal, the makeup of the village changed. Instead of providing supplies, overnight accommodations and dining opportunities, the main source of income became farming.

Frick's Lock Village outlasted the canal. The railroad, like the canal, declined, and eventually Conrail took over the tracks in 1976. Frick's Lock Village also outlasted the railroad. But then came the nuclear power station.

Frick's Lock Village remained open until the 1960s. That was when the Philadelphia Electric Company (PECO) began the construction of the Limerick Nuclear Power Station. The station was located across the Schuylkill River from Frick's Lock Village.

Federal regulations mandated that there had to be a 2,500-foot perimeter around a nuclear power station. That meant Frick's Lock Village was within that perimeter and that the residents would need to leave. PECO purchased the village, and the residents left.

Frick's Lock Village was abandoned, boarded up and at the mercy of vandals and thrill seekers. For a while, it seemed that it was destined to be demolished. That was when Paul Frick, a descendant of John Frick, began work to have the village placed in the National Register of Historical Places. He was successful, and the village was placed in the register in 2003.

In an effort to preserve the village, East Coventry Township contacted Exelon Corporation (the "new" PECO) to discuss options. As a result of negotiations, Exelon donated the village to the township and agreed to restore the village buildings.

Did You Know?

The Oldest Documented House in Chester County

The Downingtown Log House, built around 1700 by either Jeremiah Collett or Joseph Hickman, is the oldest documented house in Chester County. The house was purchased by Thomas Downing, for whom Downingtown is named, in 1739.

The building was called a log house because it had more than one floor, whereas log cabins had only one floor. It has been estimated that sixty-two trees were used in the construction of the building. This included chestnut, oak and white pine.

On the brink of falling down, an extensive renovation of the Log House took place between 1988 and 1990. This was possible through the generous donations of current and former members of the Downingtown Area Historical Society.

This is another example of the importance of preserving history. The Log House was placed in the National Register of Historic Places in 1979.

Currently, the village is fenced off with padlocked gates in an attempt to prevent further vandalism. However, the East Coventry Township Historical Commission oversees tours of the Frick's Locks Village National Historic District given by the Frick's Locks Volunteer Committee and Excelon. The East Coventry Township website (www.eastcoventry-pa.gov) lists current tour days and times.

EAST COVENTRY TOWNSHIP: SCHUYLKILL CANAL

The Schuylkill Canal came into existence due to necessity. As more people settled into the Philadelphia region, the need for more and more wood to heat homes and cook meals increased. As the need for wood increased, the availability of wood from forests in the local region declined. However, the abundance of timber in the western part of the state was known, but there were limited ways to access that timber.

Modes of transportation have evolved in the United States. First there was the horse, then the horse and cart. The iconic Conestoga wagon came next. Commercial goods traveling from Philadelphia to Pittsburgh via the Conestoga wagon took about six weeks.

Although building a canal was initially costly, once built the upkeep was minimal for the most part. It did not cost a great deal to manufacture a Conestoga wagon, but it was costly to either maintain or replace. Furthermore, the Conestoga wagon was heavy and added to the burden of transporting goods. A canalboat, on the other hand, could transport ten times its weight. At the time, canal transportation was more cost effective.

Prior to the canal being built, people would transport goods from Port Carbon to Philadelphia via boats that resembled large canoes. Because the Schuylkill River did not have a level depth, the times the river could be utilized depending on the height of the water, which usually meant having to wait until the river flooded. Hence the need for a canal with locks, so the water level could be controlled.

There existed a waterway from the interior of the state to Philadelphia, but it consisted of a non-navigable Schuylkill River. In order to access the abundant timber and coal, which people discovered could heat their homes, in Schuylkill County, the Schuylkill Canal Navigation System was incorporated in 1815. The canal was completed in 1824 and ran from Port Carbon, Pennsylvania, to Philadelphia.

Wanting to be able to move commerce more efficiently and more of it, a wide canal was proposed with barges that would be hauled by mules. The towpath for the mules followed along the banks of the canal.

With the canal being completed in 1824, the Schuylkill Navigation Company enjoyed a period of unparalleled success until 1842. This was when the Philadelphia and Reading Railroad was opened. There were benefits to a railroad that the canal did not have. The railroad still functioned even if the river froze. The railroad still functioned even if there was a drought and the water levels dropped. The railroad still functioned even if floods made the river and canal not useable.

In an attempt to compete with the railroad, which was capable of carrying more coal on average, the canal was enlarged in 1846. This increased the amount of coal that could be moved on the canal. However, due to environmental challenges such as floods and droughts, along with a coal miners' strike, the decision was made to lease the canal to the railroad.

The canal continued to transport commerce, but the tonnage continued to decline, as the railroad was able to more efficiently and cost effectively deliver coal. Finally, in 1931, the last barge made its way along the canal.

If it had not been for the Schuylkill Canal, the canal that ran through John Frick's property and the locks after which the town of Frick's Locks was named would never have come into existence.

West Bradford Township: Chester County Poorhouse/Potter's Field

The Chester County Poorhouse was Pennsylvania's first home for the poverty-stricken. It was a beautiful three-story brick house located on 350 acres. Prior to this home, the poor were cared for in private homes. And prior to that, the poor wore a red "P" on their sleeve for identification and, in many cases, for humiliation. On November 12, 1800, Indian Hannah became one of the first residents of the newly opened Chester County Poorhouse.

What made this poorhouse unique at the time was that it treated the residents with a sense of dignity and respect. There was central heat, fresh spring water and a well-equipped and well-stocked kitchen. As a form of protection, children had their own dining room and their own school.

In an effort to offset operating costs, residents worked at various jobs. There was a farm where vegetables were raised for the kitchen. Residents could chose to weave textiles and make baskets and brooms. However, the limestone quarries proved to be the best moneymaker. The lime produced was in high demand by the local farmers, which resulted in more than forty thousand bushels annually.

According to the Chester County website, "In time, the Poorhouse… would expand from one building in 1800, to include a three story brick house, barns, two infirmaries, an insane hospital, school, limestone quarry, a graveyard, smoke and bake houses, oven, wagon house, hog and slaughter house, reservoir, lake, contagious ward, stables, a two-story ward for the violently insane, calf barn, separate wings for black and white men, women, and children, and many garden and farm acres and cattle."

The poorhouse went through an evolution. Not only did it house the poor, but it also served as "an orphanage, a homeless shelter, a battered women's refuge, a lying-in hospital, a nursing home, and finally an insane asylum." The last incarnation was a state police barracks. Now the old home and outbuildings have been torn down, and a high-end housing development has been built.

The Chester County Poorhouse had three cemeteries over the history of its existence. Potter's Field Cemetery is the one best known. Prior to that, there were two other cemeteries: the Chester County Alms House Cemetery and the Chester County Home Cemetery. With the first two cemeteries full, there was a need to build the third.

Potter's Field Cemetery is located across from the Cheslen parking lot. You cross the street and go over a stone bridge. A trail through a large

The Chester County Poorhouse was Pennsylvania's first home for the poverty-stricken. It was a beautiful three-story brick building. *Courtesy of the Chester County History Center.*

meadow takes you to the cemetery, which has graves marked with a simple six-by-twelve granite stone with a number instead of a name. The numbered stones go as high as 204.

The cemetery has a white picket fence and a blue gate, which were erected by Bell Telephone volunteers who cleaned up and restored the cemetery. The volunteers made a sign to honor those who are buried there. It reads:

> *Restored*
> *Cemetery*
> *By*
> *Embreeville*
> *Center*
> *Known but to God*
> *Respected by Us*

UPPER OXFORD TOWNSHIP: HINSONVILLE

Lincoln University is known as being the first degree-granting historically Black college or university (HBCU). What most people do not know is that Lincoln University is built on the site of the village of Hinsonville—a community that was made up of free blacks and freedom seekers.

Hinsonville was named after the first permanent resident, Emory Hinson. Emory was a free black who was born in Maryland and desired to move to Pennsylvania. He purchased an eighteen-acre farm located six miles from the Mason-Dixon line separating Maryland and Pennsylvania. The first man to purchase land that was to become Hinsonville was Edward Walls, another free black man born in Maryland.

As word spread about a community of African Americans forming, free blacks wishing to leave the slave state of Maryland, as well as Chester County free blacks, moved to Hinsonville. Among the Chester County free blacks were the Amos brothers, James Ralston and Thomas Henry.

With the village of Hinsonville located a short distance from the Mason-Dixon line, residents of Hinsonville would assist freedom seekers on the road to freedom. Residents would hide them and provide them with clothing and food. There were Underground Railroad stations nearby, and freedom seekers would be brought by horse and wagon to one of those stops. Sometimes the freedom seeker, seeing the opportunities Hinsonville provided, chose to stay and assimilate into the community.

One of the members of Hinsonville who was active with the Underground Railroad was Thomas Fitzgerald. Thomas had a barn where freedom seekers coming from Virginia and Maryland could stay. Freedom seekers were welcomed by Thomas, who had one simple request: if they smoked, they were to leave their pipe and tobacco with Thomas. In the morning, the freedom seekers were provided breakfast, at which point their smoking materials were returned. If the person needed to leave before then, he would find his smoking materials outside the barn. Thomas valued his barn and did not want it accidentally burned down by careless smoking.

Hinsonville was more than just a community made up of free blacks and freedom seekers. The community was able to partake of freedoms that other small towns in Chester County enjoyed, including freedom to own land, freedom to worship, freedom to self-govern, freedom to earn a living, freedom to marry and raise a family, freedom to provide their children an education, freedom to own firearms and freedom to purchase goods and commodities.

When Emory Hinson passed away, much of his land was sold. John Powell bought thirty acres, which he sold to Reverend John Miller Dickey so Dickey could establish the Ashmun Institute, which would later be renamed Lincoln University. Ashmun Institute was cofounded by Reverend Dickey and the residents of Hinsonville, led by the Amos brothers, James Ralston and Thomas Henry. In the early days of Lincoln University, there were no dormitories, so students would board with residents of Hinsonville.

Lincoln University is the oldest degree-granting HBCU in the United States. *Courtesy of the Pennsylvania Historical and Museum Commission.*

As the university grew, so did the need for more land to expand. As more and more Hinsonville residents sold their property to the growing university, the community of Hinsonville began to disappear. Unlike other small towns throughout America, the town did not fall into decay and disappear. Instead, this small Black community was absorbed by the very university it helped found and establish.

Hinsonville existed for a short four decades. The community provided a safe place for free blacks fleeing slave states, freedom seekers who were helped by the community on their journey to freedom and freedom-seeking Blacks who settled down in the community.

KENNETT SQUARE BOROUGH: HISTORIC EAST LINDEN STREET

Historic East Linden Street is located in Kennett Square, Pennsylvania. Reportedly, this street is the oldest integrated street and the longest continually integrated street in Chester County if not the country. Established in 1846, this was fifteen years prior to the Civil War. Seventeen years after the establishment of Historic East Linden Street, President Abraham Lincoln signed the Emancipation Proclamation. Nineteen years after the establishment of Historic East Linden Street, the Thirteenth Amendment became law, freeing enslaved people.

Two local Quakers bought land that would become Historic East Linden Street. Edwin Brosius and Samuel Pennock were staunch abolitionists, agents for the Underground Railroad and highly successful businessmen. Edwin Brosius's pottery business and Samuel Pennock's agricultural machinery industry played a significant role transforming the sleepy village of Kennett Square into a thriving borough.

Edwin Brosius purchased land that would become Historic East Linden Street and built his home as well as his pottery factory. Samuel Pennock, along with his two brothers, purchased land as well. On their land they built homes for themselves as well as their employees, who worked in the Pennock Foundry, which was located a short distance from East Linden Street.

Along with Edwin Brosius and Samuel Pennock, there were other Underground Railroad agents living on East Linden Street. These included Vincent and Joanna Barnard, members of the Cox family and Levi Preston, who was Ann Preston's brother.

Conservative Quakers and progressive Quakers were a contributing factor in the establishment of East Linden Street. The issue of slavery became a point of division between the two groups. Both parties believed that slavery was wrong. The main disagreement was whether Quakers should embrace antislavery activity and, if so, what would that look like. This disagreement led to the founding of the Philadelphia Yearly Meeting of Progressive Friends, also known as the Longwood Progressive Friends Meeting (LPFM). Some of the founders of LPFM lived on Historic East Linden Street.

East Linden Street in Kennett Square, Pennsylvania, is reported to be the oldest integrated street in the United States. It has remained integrated through the present day. *Author's collection.*

Conservative Quakers believed that simply not owning slaves was enough and that they need not do anything else. Progressive Quakers believed that assistance must be given to freedom seekers in the form of the Underground Railroad and the promotion of the emancipation of enslaved people. Many of the residents of East Linden Street were not only staunch abolitionists but also progressive Quakers, and these were major contributing factors in the establishment of East Linden Street. Progressive Quakers welcomed diverse people to come and work at the two factories, as well as live on the street.

According to Dugan and Sestrich's *East Linden Street*, the 1860 census showed the diversity that existed on East Linden Street:

> *The black Veasey family lived next door to the white Prestons. African-American blacksmith Matthew Pennywell and his family lived near white master iron worker Solomon Mercer. James and Elizabeth Walker and their children were neighbors to Thomas and Eliza Millhouse. Walker, a black man, was a farm laborer, and his neighbor Millhouse, a white man, was a watchmaker. On one side of the home of Hannah Lamborn, a white woman, were the black Nicholasons, and on the other Emery and Mary Brown's family, also black.*

Likewise, the 1910 census showed

> *a mixed neighborhood with, for instance, former fugitive slave Joseph Carter living two doors from Edith Pennock of the Quaker abolitionist family. That same year, there was a string of black families living on the north side—Langs, Reeds, Cramers, Millers—and then whites: Robinsons, Prestons, Coxes, Chandlers, Grubbs.*

The diversity continues to the current time, as both Black and white families live together on the street. The diversity has expanded to include members of the Latinx community moving onto East Linden Street. This would not have been possible if it had not been for the two forward-thinking Quakers who established what is reportedly the oldest continually integrated street in the country.

WEST GROVE BOROUGH: WEST GROVE HOSPITAL

The West Grove Hospital was begun by Dr. William B. Ewing of West Grove, Pennsylvania, during the Spanish flu pandemic of 1918. Dr. Ewing first set up a small ward in a private home. Realizing that the home was too small, Dr. Ewing moved to his childhood home on Evergreen Street, West Grove. With this larger location, Dr. Ewing was able to care for five patients at a time.

Having more than five patients, the search for larger quarters began. Hearing that the Roseboro Hotel in West Grove was for sale, Dr. Ewing purchased the building, and on April 1, 1918, a twenty-bed hospital was opened. In time, this became a true community hospital, with neighbors bringing soup and other nourishment to the patients. Volunteers would provide transportation for those needing to come to the hospital.

Dr. Ewing was used to being a "country doctor," not a hospital administrator. Lacking community support initially, Dr. Ewing shouldered the financial burden of the hospital, including medical supplies and nursing salaries, as well as assuming the medical costs when poor people could not pay.

In an effort to address this issue, Dr. Ewing met with concerned citizens on May 22, 1922. The outcome of the meeting was the establishment of the Dr. Ewing Hospital Committee. The committee's first task was to figure out how to pay for charity cases. The solution was to raise an annual sum of $2,500 to pay for such cases. At this time, the committee decided to change the name of the hospital from Dr. Ewing Hospital to the West Grove Hospital.

The committee also changed its name to the West Grove Hospital Association. In an effort to encourage the community to support the hospital, "Donation Day" was begun. It was decided that this would be an annual event, which would take place the Thursday before Thanksgiving. The first Donation Day was held on Thursday, November 23, 1922.

On July 27, 1945, Dr. Ewing suffered a massive heart attack while delivering a baby. He died four days later on July 31 in the very hospital he began. When Dr. Ewing's will was read, it was discovered that he had left the hospital to the community of West Grove.

West Grove Hospital was founded by Dr. William Ewing of West Grove to meet the demands of the people affected by the Spanish flu pandemic of 1918. *Courtesy of West Grove Historian R. Scott Steele.*

Did You Know?

West Grove Had a Casket Factory

The Paxon and Comfort Casket Factory was located in West Grove, Pennsylvania. During the Spanish flu pandemic of 1918, the factory was open twenty-four hours a day in an attempt to meet the ever-increasing demand for caskets due to the many flu-related deaths. At the height of production, delivery trucks were lined up outside the factory waiting for their load of caskets to transport far and wide.

The Paxon and Comfort Company was known for high-end caskets. Due to the pandemic-related demand for caskets, a more basic wooden casket was produced. After the pandemic, high-end caskets were reintroduced and produced until the factory burned on October 11, 1929.

The Paxon and Comfort Casket Factory, although known for high-end caskets, used the West Grove factory to produce wooden caskets to meet the demand from Spanish flu–related deaths. *Courtesy of West Grove Historian R. Scott Steele.*

As early as 1922, Dr. Ewing believed that there was a need for a larger, more modern hospital in southern Chester County. At the time, there was little community interest. Dr. Ewing tried again in 1927 with no success. After World War II, a memorial hospital to honor those the soldiers who fought and survived and those who did not was proposed but failed to garner community support.

Finally, in 1954, the need for a new facility was quite apparent, and a building fund campaign was launched. The community generously responded, and a new, modern Community Memorial Hospital was completed. Unfortunately, Dr. Ewing did not live long enough to see his dream of a modern hospital being built. Without Dr. Ewing's passion, compassion and vision, it is unlikely that the new hospital would have come to fruition.

Chapter 4

SCHOOLS

NEW LONDON TOWNSHIP: NEW LONDON ACADEMY

New London Township is a small village located in southern Chester County. Driving through the township, there is a mixture of churches, businesses, farmland and a township building. The township building was home to a school that produced three signers of the Declaration of Independence and other Patriots who helped found and defend what was to become the United States of America.

New London Academy was founded by Reverend Francis Allison. It was the first public school in the colony of Pennsylvania. *Courtesy of the New London Area Historical Association.*

New London Academy was founded by Reverend Francis Alison in 1743. This was the first public school in the colony of Pennsylvania. In the early years of the school, the Philadelphia Synod of the Presbyterian Church oversaw the administration. Many ministers were trained at the school, as were politicians.

After Reverend Alison left the academy in 1752 to become vice-provost of the Philadelphia College. Alexander McDowell, who succeeded Reverend Alison, moved the academy to Newark, Delaware. McDowell's school grew into Delaware College, which later became the University of Delaware.

The New London Academy moved to Newark, Delaware, and the Newark Academy building was constructed. The Academy grew and became Delaware College, later becoming the University of Delaware. *Author's collection.*

After Alexander McDowell moved New London Academy to Newark, Delaware, the building housed the New London High School. Once the Avon Grove High School was established, the students from New London High School transferred there.

The following are students who were educated at New London Academy between 1741 and 1752, according to the *Village Record* of April 23, 1886:

> *Francis Alison, M.D., was born in Chester County. He was a surgeon in the army during the Revolution, and afterwards practiced medicine in the southern part of Chester County.*
>
> *John Bayard was a Colonel during the Revolution, and a member of the Congress of the Confederation in 1785–87.*
>
> *Matthew Brown was a member of the Provincial Conference which met in Philadelphia in June, 1776, to consider the subject of dissolving our political connection with Great Britain, and a member of the convention which framed the Pennsylvania State Constitution in 1776. He took an active part in the early stages of the Revolutionary struggle, and entered the army, but died of camp fever in 1777.*
>
> *Ephraim Blaine was prominent in the Revolutionary War and held the position of Commissary General over three years, including one of the most trying periods of the war—the cantonment of Valley Forge. He was a man of large fortune, and made considerable advances and sacrifices for the use of the patriot army, whereby his fortune was considerably impaired.*
>
> *John Cochran, M.D. studied medicine and became during the Revolution First Surgeon General of the Army of the Middle Department, and afterwards Director General of the hospitals of the United States.*
>
> *John Dickinson was delegate to Congress 1774–77 and 1779–80; President of Delaware; President and Supreme Executive Council of Pennsylvania 1782–85; delegate to the convention which framed the Constitution of the United States.*
>
> *John Hamilton served as leader of a company of calvary during the Revolution, and was out in two campaigns, those of 1776 and 1781.*
>
> *John Mackey was a member of the Continental Convention of 1776, of the Council of Safety, and of the Supreme Executive Council of Pennsylvania.*
>
> *Thomas McKean was a member of Congress; Signer of the Declaration of Independence; Chief Justice of the Supreme Court of Pennsylvania from 1777 to 1779; member of the Pennsylvania Constitutional Convention of 1790; and Governor of Pennsylvania from 1799 to 1803.*

Top: After New London Academy was moved to Newark, Delaware, the building housed New London High School. After the Avon Grove High School was built, the students went there. The building now houses the New London Township offices. *Courtesy of the New London Area Historical Association.*

Bottom: In front of the New London Academy building, there is a granite monument for the Academy. *Author's collection.*

Left: Thomas McKean, a graduate of New London Academy, was one of the signers of the Declaration of Independence and later governor of Pennsylvania. *Courtesy of the New London Area Historical Association.*

Right: Thomas McKean was a graduate of New London Academy and was one of the signers of the Declaration of Independence. *Courtesy of the Pennsylvania Historical and Museum Commission.*

Samuel Maclay was a Colonel and in active service in the Revolution; from 1792 to 1797 was an Associate Judge of Northumberland County; Member of Congress from 1795 to 1797; of the State Senate from 1797 to 1803; United States Senator from 1803 to 1809.

James McLene was a member of the Constitutional Convention of 1776; of the Assembly, 1776–77; of the Supreme Executive Council; of the Continental Congress, 1778–80; of the Council of Censors of the Constitutional Convention of 1790; and for a number of years and at different periods of the House of Representatives of Pennsylvania under the Constitution of 1790.

Robert McPherson served under General Forbes against Fort Duquesne in 1758 as Captain of Pennsylvania troops; was a Colonel during the Revolution; member of the Convention of 1776; member of the Provincial Assembly; and of the Pennsylvania Assembly, 1781–1785.

George Read was the Attorney General of Delaware; a delegate to Congress; Signer of the Declaration of Independence; Member of

Left: George Reed, a graduate of New London Academy, was one of the signers of the Declaration of Independence. *Courtesy of the New London Area Historical Association.*

Right: James Smith, a graduate of New London Academy, was one of the signers of the Declaration of Independence. *Courtesy of the New London Area Historical Association.*

Convention which framed the Constitution of the United States; United States Senator from Delaware, 1789 to 1793; and Chief Justice of Delaware.

James Smith, member of Congress and one of the Signers of the Declaration of Independence; Member of Continental Convention of 1776; Judge of the High Court of Appeals; and a Brigadier General during the Revolutionary War.

David Ramsay, M.D. was a member of the Legislature of South Carolina, 21 years; Member of Congress 1782 to 1786.

Charles Thomson was Secretary of Congress from 1774 to 1789 where his services were most efficient. John Adams, in his diary, described him as "the life of the cause of liberty."

Robert Whitehill was a member of the Convention of July 15, 1779; of the Council of Safety in 1777; of the Supreme Executive Council in 1779–81; of the Pennsylvania Assembly 1776–78 and 1784–87; of the House of Representatives of Pennsylvania under Constitution of 1790 from 1797 to 1801; of the Senate of Pennsylvania from 1801 to 1804, of which body he became Speaker; and a member of Congress from 1805 until his death in 1813.

Did You Know?

The Oldest Library in Chester County

The oldest library in Chester County is the Oxford Library. The library, begun on August 3, 1874, was originally known as the Oxford Library Company. The library was dedicated to a mission, defined by its motto: "Promise Knowledge and Literature in the Township of Oxford."

It was a subscription library with an initial membership of twenty-eight patrons. The subscription price was twenty shillings (about $2.50) and seven shillings a year thereafter. In 1868, the library opened to the public. Anyone over the age of fifteen could become a member for the nominal sum of one dollar per year. In 1939, the Oxford Library became a free library and was available to anyone wishing to access the library.

When the library opened, it had a total of 29 books. After ten years, there was a total of 121 books. After a century, the total number had grown to 1,389 books. Today, the library boasts a collection of more than 30,000 books.

Today, the Oxford Library is part of the Chester County Library System. When the library first opened, it was open for two hours in the evening. Today, it is open from Monday to Saturday.

Hugh Williamson, M.D., L.L.D. was prominent in the Revolutionary struggle and rendered essential services to the colonists in various ways.

Matthew Wilson, D.D., in the Revolution he served the patriot cause and piloted Washington when he took his position at Chadd's Ford prior to the Battle of Brandywine.

These nineteen graduates of New London Academy helped create, defend and run the young country known as the United States of America. Without New London Academy, America may never have come into existence and survived.

CHESTER SPRINGS: SOLDIERS' ORPHANS SCHOOL

The Soldiers' Orphan School system began with the election of Andrew Gregg Curtain to the office of governor of Pennsylvania in 1861. One day, he opened the door to his home only to find two children orphaned by the Civil War begging for food. He went to the state legislature to see if something could be done to assist these young people who had been left destitute by the Civil War.

Hearing of the need and wanting to help the Commonwealth of Pennsylvania provide education, room and board and daily care for orphans of Pennsylvania Civil War soldiers and sailors, the Pennsylvania Railroad Company gave the state $50,000.

According to the November 19, 1864 *Village Record*, in order to utilize the generous donation, the commonwealth legislature passed a bill on May 6, 1864, that read:

> *Children of either sex under the age of fifteen, resident of Pennsylvania at the time of application, and dependent upon either public or private charity for support, or on the exertions of a mother or other person destitute of means to afford proper education and maintenance; of fathers who have been killed, or died of wounds received, or of disease contracted in the service of the United States, whether in volunteer or militia regiments of this State, or in the regular Army or Naval service of the United States, but who were at the time of entering such service, actual bona fide residents of Pennsylvania.*

The Chester Springs Soldiers' Orphan School and Literary Institute was opened in 1869. By 1870, there were 213 students consisting of 141 boys and 72 girls. There were six grades. Subjects such as history, grammar, arithmetic, chemistry and music were studied in the higher grades. Although the governor's proclamation stated that the schools were for children under the age of fifteen, the Chester Springs Soldiers' Orphans School had what were known as the "16ers." These were children who stayed on through the age of sixteen. Even though the legislation allowed for navy and army orphans, the Chester Springs school records only list army orphans.

The typical school day ran from 8:00 a.m. until 5:00 p.m. Both boys and girls had various chores to attend to. The boys usually helped in the gardens. The girls did sewing, which included making the clothes for the girls and the shirts for the boys.

Both boys and girls wore uniforms. The girls wore dresses and sometimes skirts with a long-sleeved jacket. The boys wore a military-style uniform that was reportedly made from leftover fabric that had been used in the manufacture of Union uniforms for soldiers during the Civil War.

Male pupils at the Chester Springs Soldiers' Orphans School. *Courtesy of the Alice and David Lane Collection, Historic Yellow Springs Moore Archives.*

Etching of the Chester Springs Soldiers' Orphan School. *Courtesy of the Historic Yellow Springs Moore Archives.*

Male pupils in their uniforms, reported to have been made from leftover fabric that had been used to make Union army soldiers' uniforms. *Courtesy of the Alice and David Lane Collection, Historic Yellow Springs Moore Archives.*

At Chester Springs, there is an informative marker about the Chester Springs Soldiers' Orphan School. *Author's collection*

The boys were taught horseback riding as well as military drills, which included the use of rifles and swords. For the older male students, there was the Orphan School Band. Not only did the band perform for various school functions, but the band members also got to leave the school grounds and perform for military functions close to the school. The band would also travel to various Civil War soldiers' graves to perform on Memorial Day.

A major event that occurred annually at the school was Examination Day. This the day when politicians, local people and commonwealth school officials would come to witness the labor of the students. Plays were performed, military drills were executed, poetry was recited and students were subject to oral exams by visitors. Students proudly displayed their handwriting skills. To make sure that the students were being cared for, the facility was inspected—from the kitchen and dining hall to library, as well as student rooms—to make sure they had clean and comfortable living quarters.

When a student passed away while attending the school and had nobody to claim the body, the school provided for his or her burial at the Vincent Baptist Meeting House, located two miles away. The diseases were varied and may have included what was known back then as "wasting away disease": measles, scarlet fever, diphtheria, smallpox, typhus and yellow fever.

Did You Know?

The Chester County Mill Produced Union Army Uniforms

The Bonds' Woolen Mill (also known as the Bondsville Mill) was located on the Beaver Creek in East Brandywine Township. This mill produced a variety of textiles during its one-hundred-year existence.

Initially, the mill produced uniforms for the Union army. After the Civil War, the mill produced Kentucky jeans textile and employed more than one hundred workers. Houses were built around the mill, and the area was named Bondsville.

After World War I, the company manufactured automobile upholstery cloth. During World War II, the mill made the lining for air force jackets, also known as "Eisenhower" jackets. During this time, between three hundred and four hundred workers were employed there.

After World War II, the mill developed and produced a woven nylon material used for automobile upholstery that the company named "Candalon." Bondsville Mill closed its doors in 1954.

Today, the site has been transformed into a recreational park. The ruins of the mill are fenced off to the public because they are too unstable and dangerous. The park was opened to the public in 2015.

To obtain more information about the park and visiting hours, you can e-mail BondsvilleMill@brandywine.org or call 610-269-8230.

From 1875 until 1909, a total of twenty-one students who passed away and had nobody to claim the body were buried at the Vincent Baptist Meeting House. Nine students were female, and twelve were male. The average age at time of death was nine, with the youngest being one year of age and the oldest being sixteen years of age. The school provided the burials for these unfortunate students and placed a beautiful monument at the burial site to honor them.

After forty-three years of providing care for orphans of deceased military men, there was a decline in the need to do so, and the school closed in 1912. The remaining students were transferred to the Scotland School in Chambersburg, Pennsylvania, which closed in 2009. In 2013, the Winebrenner Theological Seminary purchased the property and had it renovated. This new school is now open to a whole new group of students.

Left: When an orphan died at the Chester County Soldiers' Orphans School and nobody came to claim the body, the child was buried at the Vincent Baptist Meeting House. *Author's collection.*

Below, left: From 1875 to 1909, twenty-one students passed away at the Chester County Soldiers' Orphans School who had nobody to claim the bodies and were buried in a cemetery plot the school had purchased for these students. *Author's collection.*

Below, right: Architectural headstone for the Vincent Baptist Meeting House, where the Chester County Soldiers' Orphans School burial plot is located. *Author's collection.*

TREDYFFRIN TOWNSHIP: DIAMOND ROCK OCTAGONAL SCHOOL

Near Paoli, Pennsylvania, there are the North Valley Hills of Tredyffrin Township, Chester County, where large boulders contain a crystallized quartz that can, like diamonds, cut glass. The geological formation is believed to be the only known formation like it in the world. Prior to the increase in settlers and construction of homes, people could see the "diamonds" shimmering in the light that fell on the boulders. These quartz crystals were sold to jewelers in Philadelphia, who would cut and polish them to be used in various types of jewelry.

Early on in the history of the colonies, both the Friends and the Presbyterians, believing in the importance of education, set aside rooms in their meetinghouses and churches to provide education. As the demand for education grew, the need for actual schools with it.

Llewellyn David, one of the six Welsh David brothers who immigrated with their father to the colonies, purchased land situated in Tredyffrin that was part of the Welsh Tract. Ann Llewellyn, the daughter of Llewellyn

The Diamond Rock Octagonal School by 1905 was in dire need of restoration and repair. *Courtesy of the Chester County History Center.*

David, married George Beaver. George believed in the importance of education and donated land on which to build a school for local youths.

The school was built on land that was at the foot of the Diamond Rocks. The shape of the school was octagonal, which was chosen as a preferred construction design for a few reasons: there could be more windows as opposed to a four-corner design, the students had better access to the stove in the center of the room and the school master sitting in the center of the room had better supervision of his or her students than in a square design. The name of the school came from being close to the Diamond Rocks and being octagonal in shape.

In 1813, the Diamond Rock Octagonal School opened its doors to students. At any given time, up to sixty-five students were in attendance. There were desks and benches for the students. When seated, the students' backs were toward the center of the room, where the stove was located. The older children attended during the winter months, with the younger children attending during the warmer spring and fall months.

The basic curriculum at the school consisted of the traditional "three Rs": reading, writing and 'rithmetic. As was typical of schools at this time, there were no formal grades. Every student was a grade unto himself. In additional to the basics, the teacher would add knowledge from the book or books students brought from home. The boys also learned surveying, and the girls learned embroidery.

Historical plaque for the Diamond Rock Octagonal School, placed by the Tredyffrin Township Historical Commission. *Author's collection.*

One funny story came out of the school. Being impressed with how the older students were progressing with their basic studies, the teacher decided that it might be time to introduce a new topic. Students went home and told their parents about this new topic. There followed an uproar in the community. Concerned parents met with the school board, which in turn met with the teacher. Board members informed the teacher that religion (sin) and politics (taxes) had no place in their school. Wisely realizing that this was a losing battle, the teacher conceded to their wishes. Rather than try to explain what syntax was, the teacher simply discontinued the lessons.

The Diamond Rock Octagonal School in the present day—fully restored. *Author's collection.*

The school served the educational needs of the community from 1818 until 1864, when public schools began being built in Pennsylvania. For many years, the school sat vacant, exposed to the weather and vandals. By 1905, the school had become a total wreck, with broken windows and no roof.

Former students of the school, as well as other concerned citizens, realized that the school was in dire need of repair. A restoration association was formed, and work began on the school, ending in 1918, when the newly restored school reopened. Due to the efforts of these local citizens, Diamond Rock Octagonal School is believed to be the only surviving octagonal school in the country.

This is an example of what happens when people realize that a historic structure is on the verge of disappearing and take action. Not only is there unknown, little-known and forgotten history in Chester County, but there is also history that has been preserved.

DOWNINGTOWN: DOWNINGTOWN INDUSTRIAL AND AGRICULTURAL SCHOOL

The Downingtown Industrial and Agricultural School (DIAS), located in Downingtown, Pennsylvania, was founded in 1904 by Reverend William A. Creditt. Reverend Creditt was the pastor of the First African Baptist Church, located in Philadelphia. John Trower, a wealthy businessman, was a member of the First African Baptist Church. Trower provided the funds to purchase the 110-acre McFarlan Farm on which DIAS was built.

Both men believed in the importance of providing young African American children with an education that would provide worthwhile employment, while keeping young people off the streets to prevent them from becoming juvenile delinquents. The men received their inspiration to found the school by the example of Booker T. Washington, who in 1881 founded the Tuskegee Normal and Industrial Institute in Tuskegee, Alabama.

The school was coeducational and served students in grades six through twelve. The motto of the school was "Self-Help through Self-Worth." The school's founders wanted to provide education for African American youth, who were neglected and struggling in school. As a means to achieve these goals, both teachers and students lived on campus.

Because the school was focusing on agricultural and industrial education, students not only studied the basics—reading, writing and

Did You Know?

Boarding School for Boys

In the August 13, 1834 edition of the *American Republic*, Joshua Hoopes announced that he was proposing to open a school for boys and young gentlemen in the town of West Chester, Pennsylvania.

The West Chester Boarding School for Boys (also known as the Hoopes Boarding School) was built in 1836 as a private academy. Courses offered included French, English, Latin, Greek, basic math, geometry and algebra. Boys could also study history, astronomy and surveying.

The annual cost for the school was $160, which included schooling and room and board. Students were required to provide their own wash basins and towels.

Students were given two weeks off in the spring and the fall; however, school instruction continued during these times, and students were responsible for keeping up with their caseload. If a student did take either two-week break, there was a reduction in the cost of the schooling. Students were also required to attend the house of worship their parents designated for them.

The West Chester Boarding School for Boys closed in 1862.

arithmetic—but there were also a variety of other courses. These included carpentry, plumbing, automotive technology, home economics, typing and business training.

As part of the agricultural training, students helped raise fruits and vegetables and took care of the chickens and cows that provided the school with milk and eggs. To aid students build their self-worth, topics such as personal hygiene, public speaking and how to be more self-assured were covered. Some students focused on academic studies and took advantage of college prep course, and in 1912, fifteen DIAS graduates headed to Lincoln University to pursue higher education.

Reverend Creditt was the brother of Anna Creditt (Reed), who was the maternal grandmother of Cab Calloway. This is significant because in 1921, Cab Calloway's parents, concerned with Cab's school delinquency and horse gambling, sent Cab to DIAS.

Calloway was enrolled at the school for about a year. Calloway is quoted as saying, "That year in Downingtown made a big difference. I walked into Downingtown a little boy, and I came out a man. What made the difference

Left: The Downingtown Industrial and Agricultural School closed in 1993. In 1999, Delaware Community College purchased the property. *Author's collection.*

Below: A plaque honoring the Downingtown Industrial and Agricultural School was placed at the Downingtown Campus of Delaware County Community College in 2021. *Author's collection.*

SITE OF DOWNINGTOWN INDUSTRIAL AND AGRICULTURAL SCHOOL

The school was established in 1904 by William A. Creditt, Pastor of Philadelphia's First African Baptist Church, who was inspired by the work of Booker T. Washington and his funding of the Tuskegee Institute in Alabama in 1881. The mission of the school was to help Black students develop skills to earn a livelihood through the teaching of agriculture, mechanical trades, and domestic arts, along with basic education.

The initial benefactor of this effort was John Trower, a member of Creditt's church, considered one of the wealthiest African Americans in the United States. Trower's success in the catering business enabled him to purchase the McFarlan Farm, 110 acres on the north side of Horseshoe Pike, and the Downingtown Industrial and Agricultural School opened with 30 male and female students in grades 6 through 12. Creditt served as the first principal, and teachers and students lived on the campus with the school adopting the motto of "self-help through self-worth."

In addition to academics, classes were offered in carpentry, plumbing, auto mechanics, home economics, typing and business training. Most of the fruits, vegetables, eggs and milk were raised or grown on campus. Sports programs were developed in the late 1920s along with programs to aid in poise and self-assurance, public speaking, grooming, scouting, chorus and public debate. During the war years students received instruction in first aid, military drill, and civil defense.

The school experienced a devastating fire in 1946 but continued to provide educational and child services in various forms until 1993. Delaware County Community College purchased the site in 1999 and opened this campus in 2002.

was being away from home [Baltimore, Maryland] and having to make it on my own….Downingtown was a turning point for me."

DIAS continued to provide African American youth with a worthwhile education until 1993. The site sat vacant until 1999, at which time Delaware County Community College purchased the property. In 2002, the Downingtown Campus of Delaware County Community College opened its doors to provide a new group of students a quality education.

On September 30, 2021, alumni of the former DIAS came to together with Delaware County Community College leaders. This was an opportunity for alumni to share stories about their experiences while at DIAS and to have their DIAS memories recorded for future generations.

The college, along with the East Brandywine Township Historical Commission, planned the alumni reunion along with a plaque unveiling. The historic plaque provides Delaware County Community College students the opportunity to learn about the rich heritage that came prior to DCCC.

Chapter 5
MANUFACTURING

OXFORD: OXFORD CARAMEL FACTORY

Since 1882, W.F. Parker owned and operated a caramel factory in Philadelphia. Faced with high milk costs in the city (the factory used between four thousand and six thousand quarts daily) and the high cost of running his business, Mr. Parker began looking for alternatives,

When the Oxford Land and Improvement Company was formed, it included bankers and merchants. Established in 1891, the goal was to attract new business to Oxford, Pennsylvania. With money raised by selling bonds, the company purchased a large parcel of land. New companies coming to Oxford would receive tax breaks and assistance with the construction of their businesses.

W.F. Parker heard about Oxford and the favorable business climate. He and his brother, Charles M., who was also his business partner, ended up purchasing two lots. Having made the decision to move the caramel factory to Oxford, the Parker brothers hired Milton Walker to build their new business, which included a railroad siding to make shipping product easier.

The company began production in April 1892 as the W.F. Parker and Company until 1894, when it was incorporated as the Oxford Caramel Company. The company building consisted of two stories. The second floor housed the equipment to manufacture the candy, and the first floor housed the packing and wrapping department.

The Oxford Caramel Company produced six tons of candy per week. The candy production staff was made up of women as well as girls age sixteen to eighteen. *Courtesy of the Oxford Area Historical Association.*

The building was very modern for the time. Steam heat flowed through eleven thousand feet of pipe. The company generated its own electricity to provide lighting and run the equipment. Along with generating its own steam and electricity, it also produced its own boxes and candy wrappers. That meant there was no need to worry about a middle man and reduced profits.

Other than the supervisors and maintenance men, the candy production staff was made up of women, as well as girls who ranged from sixteen to eighteen years of age. The factory produced six tons of candy, both caramels and chocolate, per week. In the first six months of operation, the factory produced 550 tons of candy and used 200,000 gallons of milk.

The Oxford Caramel Factory product was shipped throughout the United States and internationally, including the countries of Canada, Ireland, England, South America, Mexico and Australia. Oxford was considered the trade center between Baltimore and Philadelphia. This was further strengthened with the introduction of the railroad to Oxford in 1860. The two main railroads that ran through Oxford were the Philadelphia, Wilmington and Baltimore Line and the narrow-gauge Lancaster, Oxford and Southern Railroad.

Business continued to grow, and Milton Walker was rehired to build a large warehouse later in 1892. With increased business, the number of employees increased from 150 to 500 workers. In 1907, the company changed its name to the Williams Caramel Company, and then in 1910, it became the Oxford Confectionary.

The Depression had an adverse impact on the company, and the decision was made to put the company up for sale. A local businessman, John H. Ware Jr., purchased the company. In spite of Mr. Ware's hard work and determination, the sale of candy did not do well, and the Oxford Confectionary Company closed its doors in 1933.

The building was eventually reopened as the Oxford Furniture Company, followed by the Oxford Cabinet Company. In 1947, a fire destroyed the building.

For forty-one years, the Oxford Caramel Factory produced caramels, chocolates and confectionery products known throughout the United States and many countries in the world.

PHOENIXVILLE: THE GRIFFEN CANNON

The Phoenix Iron Company, located in Phoenixville, Pennsylvania, in southern Chester County, was well known for the production of building materials for skyscrapers, bridges and railroads. Less known was the piece of equipment that many historians believe changed the course of the Civil War. The three-inch ordnance rifle, Model 1861, better known as the Griffen gun or Griffen cannon. This cannon was used more than any other during the Civil War.

Prior to John Griffen developing the Griffen cannon, the average field artillery piece weighed 988 pounds, making it more difficult to transport. The Griffen only weighed 620 pounds. In 1854, Mr. Griffen wondered if a field gun could be made from wrought iron. He did not think it was possible due to the possibility of the gun splitting upon firing. Then he had the idea to have the cannon equipped in the same manner as a rifle—that is, with a rifle bore.

Mr. Griffen received permission from the company to pursue his idea, and a sample gun was manufactured. The gun was sent for government testing. The standard test meant firing the new gun three times with a two-pound cannonball. If it did not split open during this test, it was accepted by the government.

The standard test of three shots was completed, the gun passed and Mr. Griffen was asked if he was satisfied with the results. Mr. Griffen told the people in charge of testing to continue firing until the cannon burst. The typical life of a cannon at that time was five hundred charges, or shots.

After five hundred charges, the test cannon was examined, and it was discovered that the barrel had not been affected at all. But the testing did not stop there. Further charges were applied to the cannon until finally the cannon was filled with seven pounds of charge and thirteen cannonballs. The cannon was shot with a deafening roar, and the cannon finally burst. Mr. Griffen's rifle bore design for the Griffen cannon proved a huge success.

The federal government, impressed with the results, placed an initial order with the Phoenix Iron Company for three hundred guns. By the end of the Civil War, according to army records, at least nine hundred guns had been purchased. By 1863, 40 percent of the Army of the Potomac's artillery inventory consisted of the Griffen cannon.

On July 1, 1863, a Griffen cannon, under the direction of General John Buford's order, fired the first shot of the Battle of Gettysburg, the battle that many historians believed changed the course of the war in favor of the Union, thus preventing the northern expansion of the Confederate army.

At the time of the Civil War, cannons were mounted on horse-drawn carriages. Due to the lighter weight of the cannon, the cannon artillerymen could keep pace with cavalrymen.

Today, if you tour the Gettysburg Battlefield and go to General Buford's Monument, you can see the Griffen cannon that shot the opening salvo of the Battle of Gettysburg. In addition to the Buford cannon, there are more than seventy-five Griffen cannons located throughout the Gettysburg Battlefield grounds at their original battle locations.

The Battle of Gettysburg took place in 1863. To celebrate Armed Forces Day in Phoenixville, Pennsylvania, in 1963, a fully restored Griffen cannon was housed in a twenty-square-foot stone building that has glass on three sides at Reeves Park in Phoenixville. The cannon is still housed there, and you can stop by Reeves Park to view it.

The Griffen cannon, produced by the Phoenix Iron Company, played a major role in the Union army, helping to win the Civil War. *Courtesy of the Pennsylvania Historical and Museum Commission.*

A Griffen cannon under the direction of General John Buford's order fired the first shot of the Battle of Gettysburg. Many historians believe that the Griffen cannon was a major factor in the Union winning the Civil War. *Courtesy of the Historical Society of the Phoenixville Area.*

Did You Know?

The Phoenix Iron Company Monorail

The first monorail was made in Phoenixville, Pennsylvania, by the Phoenix Iron Company. It may also have been the first monorail exhibited at a world's fair.

The monorail was produced for the Centennial Exhibition of 1876, located at Fairmont Park in Philadelphia, Pennsylvania. This Centennial Celebration turned out to be the first world's fair held in the United States.

The monorail designed and built by the Phoenix Iron Company went by a variety of names, such as the Peg-Leg Railroad, the Single Railroad and the Safety Railroad.

The Centennial monorail was set up for demonstration purposes, and the track was only five hundred feet long. However, the monorail was able to demonstrate that it was safe, practical and economic, thus paving the way for future monorails found throughout the world today.

The first monorail was made in Phoenixville, Pennsylvania, by the Phoenix Iron Company. *Courtesy of the Historical Society of the Phoenixville Area.*

In his Gettysburg Address, President Abraham Lincoln said, "The world will little note, nor long remember what we say here, but it can never forget what they did here." Had it not been for the Griffen cannon, the outcome of the Civil War may have taken a totally different turn, and Lincoln may never have had the opportunity to deliver his Gettysburg Address.

PHOENIXVILLE: ETRUSCAN MAJOLICA

John Griffen, developer of the Griffen cannon and a superintendent at the Phoenix Iron Company, had been in a dispute over patent rights to the cannon. In 1862, dissatisfied with the outcome of the patent argument, he resigned from the company and moved out of state. The Phoenix Iron Company was able to persuade Mr. Griffen to return to the company five years later.

In the meantime, both of John's sons, George and Henry, had graduated from college. Still upset about the patent dispute, John refused to allow his sons to work for the company.

Instead, he remained at Phoenix Iron Company and purchased a pottery business for his sons. To assist his sons, John hired William Smith and William Hill, both of whom had experience in the pottery business. The company was named Griffen, Smith and Hill.

The pottery produced by these men was called "Etruscan Majolica," and on the bottom of the pieces there was the monogram "G.S. and H." Seeing where people enjoyed English china and pottery, the company used the name "Etruscan" as an homage to Wedgwood's Etruria line of china.

Many firms in the United States attempted to manufacture majolica between the years of 1846 and 1881. Griffen, Smith and Hill was the only truly successful company. The company was based in Phoenixville. The Historical Society of the Phoenixville Area is home to the largest collection of Etruscan Majolica in the United States.

The World's Industrial and Cotton Centennial Exposition of 1884 was held in New Orleans. The Griffen, Smith and Hill company entered some of its pieces in the exposition and won a gold medal for two vases and a jug. Due to this new notoriety, the company had an influx of new orders for its pottery, which help the company grow and expand.

Another way the company gained national recognition was when the Atlantic and Pacific Tea Company (A&P) used Etruscan Majolica as premiums to induce current and potential customers to shop at its stores.

At the World's Industrial and Cotton Centennial Exposition of 1884, Griffen, Smith and Hill Company entered some of its Etruscan Majolica. Two vases and one jug won gold medals. *Courtesy of the Historical Society of the Phoenixville Area.*

Girls were trained to paint the Etruscan Majolica. In this picture, the two gentlemen seated in the front are George and Henry, the sons of John Griffen, the founder of Etruscan Majolica. *Courtesy of the Historical Society of the Phoenixville Area.*

The daughter of one of the partners in the Etruscan Company had a pet cat pass away. The cat was taken to a taxidermist, who removed the bones, which were ground to provide the powder to make a bone china tea cup—called the "Cat Cup." *Courtesy of the Historical Society of the Phoenixville Area.*

This resulted in Phoenixville Etruscan Majolica being spread throughout the country.

By 1886, Etruscan Majolica was at peak production. After the pottery was made and fired in the huge kiln, it needed to be decorated. This was accomplished by twenty girls, who had been trained by expert artists. The girls would hand-decorate the various pieces, which depicted among other things birds, fish, flowers, shells and vegetables.

One of the more unusual pieces on display at the Historical Society of Phoenixville Area's Etruscan Majolica collection is a piece of bone china called the "Cat Cup." William Smith, one of the partners in Griffen, Smith and Hill, had a daughter, Alice, who had a pet cat. When the cat died in 1879, Alice took the cat to a taxidermist. The taxidermist removed the cat's bones, which were then ground into a powder. Alice brought the powder to the majolica plant, where there was just enough of the bone powder to make one bone china tea cup.

The company continued to expand until, at the height of its success, there was a major fire in 1890, at which time the factory closed. There were various attempts to reopen as a pottery/china company, but none was successful, resulting in the kilns and manufacturing sites being torn down. After sitting vacant for a number of years, a senior housing complex was built on the land.

PHOENIXVILLE: PHOENIX COLUMNS AND THE WASHINGTON MONUMENT

Along with the Statue of Liberty, the Washington Monument is one of the most recognizable monuments in the world. It is the tallest obelisk in the world. Each year, close to 500,000 people visit the Washington Monument. However, most of those visitors do not know the unknown history surrounding the structure itself.

The Phoenix Column was invented by Samuel Reeves in 1862. The column is hollow inside and consists of pieces that are riveted together. An advantage of the hollow columns was they were lighter and stronger than solid cast-iron columns. The fact that the columns were constructed of wrought-iron pieces riveted together meant that beams could be attached to the column where the rivets were connected.

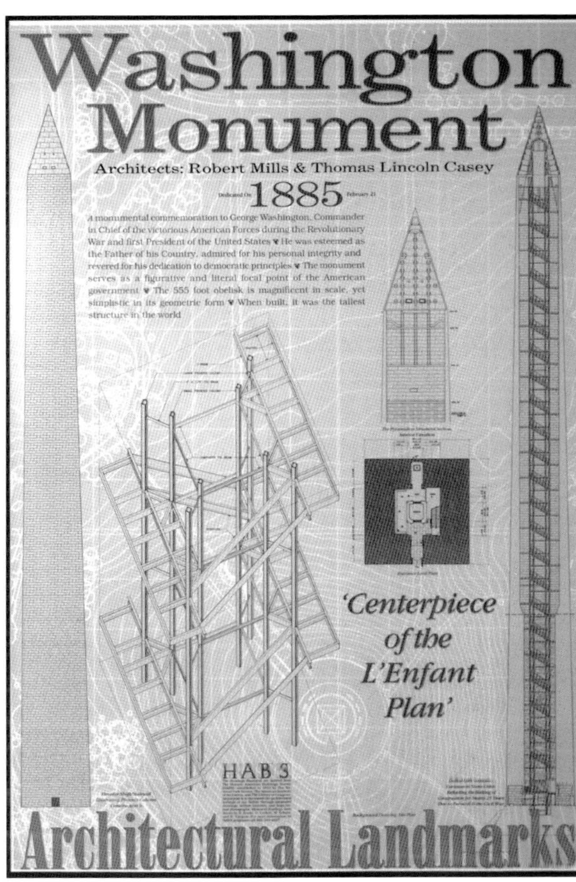

Opposite: Construction of the Washington Monument showing Phoenix Columns, which were used throughout the monument. *Courtesy of the Historical Society of the Phoenixville Area.*

Left: This poster was used to promote the Washington Monument. It shows the Phoenix Columns used in the construction of the structure. *Courtesy of the Historical Society of the Phoenixville Area.*

The invention of the Phoenix Column, produced by the Phoenix Iron Works based in Chester County, dramatically changed the landscape of the American skyline. Actual skyscrapers could now truly be built. No longer were civil engineers tied to the current construction design of a square box-like building—rectangular buildings could be built.

Inside the Washington Monument, there was a total of eight Phoenix Columns—four for the elevator shaft and four for the stairwell. The stairwell was built of four Phoenix Columns laid out in a fifteen-foot square with a column at each corner. Within this square the elevator shaft was built with four Phoenix Columns placed at each corner of a nine-and-a-half-foot square. The elevator columns were attached to the stairwell columns.

During the construction of the monument, all eight columns were purposely higher than the stone obelisk. This provided support for the cranes that brought the stone blocks up to be placed on the shaft as it was being built. The finished columns, when assembled by riveting the pieces together, reached a height of five hundred feet.

The four outer stairwell columns weigh more than the four elevator columns. This means that the outer columns provided the strength to support the inner columns.

The Washington Monument is listed in the National Register of Historic Places. It has also been designated a Historic Civil Engineering Landmark by the American Society of Civil Engineers.

VALLEY FORGE PARK: COLONIAL SPRINGS BOTTLING PLANT

Valley Forge National Park has many historic places that the visitor should see, including Washington's Headquarters, the Muhlenberg Brigade Huts, the National Memorial Arch and the Washington Memorial Chapel. One place many visitors have not seen nor are even aware exists is the Colonial Springs Bottling Plant.

Exactly when the spring water began to be bottled commercially is not known, but many believe that it may have been when the property was purchased in 1895 by General Benjamin Franklin Fisher. Fisher was part of the Signal Corps during the Civil War. During one of his reconnaissance maneuvers, he was captured by the Confederates and sent to Libby Prison in Richmond, Virginia.

Fisher managed to escape and was able to return to the North. Considered a hero by many, he was promoted to chief signal officer of the U.S. Army. Following his time with the army, he moved near Valley Forge and, along with his brother, purchased land on Mount Misery. In 1895, Fisher purchased a tract of land that contained the Colonial Springs.

In 1900, a gentleman by the name of C.T. Chase and Fisher entered into a business arrangement whereby Chase would purchase five thousand gallons or more of the water from Cold Springs. Prior to being known as Colonial Springs, the site was known as Cold Springs. In 1908, the Colonial Springs Company leased water rights of Cold Springs from Fisher.

From 1908 until about 1930, the Colonial Spring Bottling Company water was sold throughout southeastern Pennsylvania. For a fee, the company would make home deliveries of the spring water. Colonial Springs water was very popular in Philadelphia. Other people, wanting to enjoy a ride in the country, would venture to the bottling plant, where they were allowed to

Inside the ruins of the Colonial Springs Bottling Plant. *Author's collection.*

Top: Doorway to the ruins of the Colonial Springs Bottling Plant. *Author's collection.*

Bottom: This is the actual spring of the Colonial Springs Bottling Company. The spring is still active today. *Author's collection.*

Opposite: Entrance to the spring of the Colonial Springs Bottling Plant. *Author's collection.*

bottle their own water at no cost. The land that housed the bottling plant was purchased by the National Park Service in 1930, and the Colonial Springs Bottling Plant stopped production.

If you want to visit the remains of the Colonial Springs Bottling Plant, you can reach it by hiking. From Washington's Headquarters, you can hike the Chapel Trail, cross over Route 23, go to the Horse Shoe Trail and then branch off onto the Mount Misery Trail. As you climb the Mount Misery Trail, you will come across a stone building whose roof has long deteriorated. This is the remains of the Colonial Springs Bottling Plant.

What is amazing is that the springs are still running. As you start up the Mount Misery Trail, you will see water running down on the right-hand side. Once you go through the doorway of the plant, you will see an archway straight ahead. If you go inside the cave-like structure, you will see water bubbling up from the ground.

OXFORD: NARROW-GAUGE RAILROAD

In the early days of railroading, there were two types of railroad tracks: the standard gauge and the narrow gauge. The standard gauge was first used by Englishman George Stephenson, who designed and built the first steam locomotive. The railroad tracks he had laid down for his train were based on the width of the coal wagons in the region. This width was also based on the distance between Roman chariot wheels, which was four feet, eight and a half inches. When England was conquered by the Romans, the Romans brought their chariots with them. The indentations left by the chariots became the standard first for wagons and then for railroads in England.

Railroads were first built in England, and American engineers traveled to England to learn about railroads. In England, the engineers learned about the Stephenson standard gauge. When the American engineers arrived home, the Stephenson gauge was adopted as the norm, although some railroads utilized the narrow gauge for different reasons.

Narrow-gauge railroad tracks were popular in mountainous regions, where there were tighter curves. Narrow gauge was also popular because it cost less to build and maintain. A downside of narrow gauge was that less freight could be transported, and narrow-gauge locomotives were not as fast as standard-gauge locomotives. Furthermore, narrow-gauge trains were usually limited in their travels because a third rail would need to be added to accommodate the narrower train.

The Lancaster, Oxford and Southern Railroad (LOS) came into existence through a series of bankruptcies. The first railroad was built between 1872 and 1878. It was known as the Eastern Division of the Peach Bottom Railway. The rail line ran between Oxford and Peach Bottom.

The main source of revenue was passenger business and freight from farms along the line. At the time, there were no industries that could provide financial support to the railroad. The Peach Bottom Railway went bankrupt in 1881 and became the Peach Bottom Railroad.

After the railroad went bankrupt in 1890, investors purchased the company, and it became Lancaster, Oxford and Southern Railroad. Originally, the investors planned to convert the narrow-gauge rail system to standard gauge, but the finances were lacking.

Again, there was not enough income to support the company, and in 1911, the company went bankrupt. In 1912, the company became the LOS and was in operation from 1912 until 1918. In 1914, the railway was sold again due to continued financial difficulties.

The new owners tried to streamline operations, to no avail. The advent of the trucking industry meant that farmers did not have to transport their goods to railway crossings to be picked up. Trucks could carry loads to varied locations more easily than the train. Added to this was the World War I demand for scrap metal. These two factors led to the LOS closing for good in 1918.

In September 1918, the railroad tracks, engines, railroad cars and railroad bridges were all sold for scrap metal. The rights of way that crossed various pieces of land were returned to the landowners. Fortunately, all financial obligations were able to be met, and investors were paid.

The LOS was originally going to be a standard-gauge railway; however, it appeared to be more financially expedient to make it a narrow-gauge railroad, as narrow-gauge railroads are less expensive to build and operate than standard gauge. Unfortunately, the narrow-gauge played a major role in the demise of the LOS.

The first passenger train station in Oxford was built around 1860. Shortly after, the first freight depot was built close by. In order to accommodate the LOS, along with standard-gauge railroads, a third rail was added.

Oxford was where the LOS and the Philadelphia and Baltimore Central Railroad met. This meant that any freight aboard the LOS needed to be unloaded and transferred from the narrow-gauge cars to the standard-gauge cars of the Philadelphia and Baltimore Central Railroad. This meant that goods were handled three times rather than once.

Narrow-gauge railroad cars were not as large as standard gauge and therefore were not capable of carrying as much freight. With the dawn of the trucking industry came a more efficient manner of transporting goods. The LOS was limited where it could go simply by the tracks it ran on. Instead of a farmer having to take his goods to the train station to be picked up, he could wait for the truck to come to him.

Above: Railroad track had to include a third rail to accommodate the narrow-gauge Lancaster, Oxford and Southern Railroad. *Courtesy of the Oxford Area Historical Association.*

Left: Prior to railroad track width regulation, some railroad chose to utilize the narrow-gauge track format, as it cost less to build and maintain. *Courtesy of the Oxford Area Historical Association.*

DID YOU KNOW?

THE FIRST AUTOMOBILE IN CHESTER COUNTY

Burton Murdaugh built the first automobile in Chester County. Murdaugh owned a bicycle shop in Oxford, Pennsylvania. In 1900, Murdaugh bought a kit from which he was able to assemble his first of three cars.

The cars consisted of four bicycle wheels, a one-cylinder engine and bicycle chains to power the wheels. With such little power produced by the small engine, people riding their bicycles had fun "outrunning" the slow automobile.

Oxford residents often remembered seeing Mr. Murdaugh walking back to his shop after his car malfunctioned. In spite of the shortcomings of his automobile, Mr. Murdaugh could lay claim to being the builder of the first automobile in Chester County, which he was willing to sell to anyone willing to pay $600.

The Murdaugh automobile was the first car built in Chester County. *Courtesy of the Oxford Area Historical Association.*

The Lancaster, Oxford and Southern Railway (LOS) was also popular with young people, who enjoyed playing the LOS game. *Courtesy of the Oxford Area Historical Association.*

The LOS was known as "Little, Old, and Slow," "Peachy," "Narrow Gauge" and "Lost and Out of Sight." The LOS was a down-home railroad. Although the railroad had purchased rights of way from farmers, many farmers kept their fences where they had always been. This resulted in the train having to stop and the fence rails being moved to the side. Once the train went through the opening, the fence rails would have to be put back to prevent cows from escaping.

The LOS was, in many ways, similar to the carousel at the carnival where children would lean out to grab the ring. Farmers would tie produce or animals to fenceposts along the line for the train to pick up. Likewise, people would secure mail and packages to fenceposts as well to be picked up by the train.

The life of the LOS was short, as was the distance of its reach—never more than twenty-eight miles. So, in 1918, the only narrow-gauge railroad in Chester County ceased to exist. The LOS was more than a railroad. It was a popular attraction beloved by children and adults.

WEST CHESTER: SILK PRODUCTION

China is known for its silk and the monopoly it held on silk production for centuries. Less known is how, in the 1830s, a plan was put in place to turn West Chester, Pennsylvania, into a thriving center of silk production.

Silk production originated in China and eventually spread throughout Europe, with France and Italy becoming the leading producers of silk. The "silk road" traveled across the Atlantic, and one of the places it landed was Pennsylvania. William Penn and Benjamin Franklin were strong advocates for the production of silk. By the mid-1700s, silk was being cultivated by a handful of farmers in Chester County, producing minimal amounts.

Even though the annual production was not great, there were a few prominent Chester County businessmen who took notice and wondered if a detailed, comprehensive plan to cultivate mulberry trees and silkworms might lead to further wealth. In the 1830s, these men began their quest to make West Chester an epicenter of silk production.

Charles Miner was the editor of the West Chester newspaper the *Village Record*. Miner was a huge proponent of silk production, which he promoted in his hometown newspaper and Washington, D.C., where he was a congressman. He laid out a comprehensive plan to cultivate mulberry trees (of which he was willing to donate a thousand) and silkworms. His plan never came to fruition due to his declining health.

Miner's quest for a silk production empire was taken up by John Rutter. Rutter was a practicing lawyer, but his avocation was horticulture. True to his interests, Rutter was the president of the Chester County Horticultural Society.

Under Rutter's guidance, the Chester County Silk Company was formed in 1836. The sale of shares in the company raised needed capital. The company purchased land, planted mulberry trees, released silkworms and waited for the cocoons to develop. Much of the nation was enamored of the possibility of the silk production get-rich scheme. Some of the farmers who had early on raised mulberry trees and produced modest amounts of silk suddenly became the experts in how to be a part of the silk production mania.

One such "expert" was one of original silk farmers Chester County. Mr. Mahan's newspaper was called the *Silk Grower's Instructor and Farmer's Friend*. In this monthly newspaper were get-rich stories. As is often the case with "it sounds good to be true" situations, most of the people who tried their hand at silk production did not get rich.

The Chester County Silk Company purchased a number of mulberry trees, including the Chinese mulberry tree and the Italian mulberry tree. Hundreds of mulberry trees, of both varieties, were planted. Next came the silkworms.

According to a *Village Record* article from September 25, 1838, "Several gentlemen have made fortunes, Mr. Rutter, of our borough [West Chester]… has made a very handsome income." Looking to get rich quick, people were buying mulberry trees at inflated rates.

The mounting operating costs outweighed the silk produced. As it turned out, there more mulberry trees in supply than demand. Fortunately, the Chester County Silk Company had only partially invested in Chinese mulberry trees, so in 1838, the company was able to temporarily remain solvent.

Then came the 1839 financial crash, which ended the quest for silk production dominance in West Chester. In 1840, 2,500 Chinese mulberry trees, which only a few years ago were selling for inflated prices, were now selling for cents on the dollar. Shortly thereafter, the trees were being given away, as nobody was willing to pay for them.

The Chester County Silk Company had dreamed of turning West Chester into a major center for silk production. Despite its efforts, the lower-than-expected output from the silkworms and the economic downturn shattered that dream. The quest for silk production dominance came to an end.

Chapter 6

ENTERTAINMENT AND RECREATION

WEST CHESTER: LENAPE PARK

If you are driving to West Chester on Route 52, you will cross over the Brandywine River. Looking to your left as you cross over the bridge, you will see the remains of what used to be a popular recreational park: Lenape Park.

The origins of Lenape Park began in 1891. The West Chester Street Railway Company ran a trolley from West Chester to Lenape. The railroad and trolley company management realized that there was an untapped revenue source that was a parcel of land between the Lenape trolley station and the picturesque Brandywine Creek.

Work began on the property, and by the summer of 1892, there were a variety of attractions including "a picnic ground, a boardwalk, boating wharf, dance pavilion, and a carousel." After building a dam across the Brandywine Creek, a man-made beach and lake were created. Trolley riders began to compare Lenape Park to the likes of Atlantic City or Coney Island.

Lenape Park became popular, as the attendance numbers can attest—900 visitors on one day visited the park in 1892. The one-day number in 1906 topped 4,000 to 5,000, and by mid-twentieth century, more than 200,000 people visited the park in one season.

In order to continue to attract visitors, new attractions were added. A merry-go-round was added that in the beginning was turned by farm boys. The boys were replaced by horses, and as technology improved, the power came from a gas-powered engine and then an electric one.

One of the most popular rides at Lenape Park was the roller coaster, which stood 50 feet high and had 1,400 feet of track. *Courtesy of the Chester County History Center.*

The merry-go-around was added in 1926. Lenape Park hired Gustav and William Dentzel to build the merry-go-round. This magnificent work of art consisted of hand-carved animals, including horses, tigers, lions and giraffes. The music for this masterpiece was provided by a Wurlitzer Band organ.

One of the most popular rides was added in 1926. This was a roller coaster that stood 50 feet high and had 1,400 feet of track. Also popular were the miniature golf course and the bumper cars.

Lenape Park provided entertainment and diversion from life's problems during the Depression and World War II. Picnics were popular at the park. Families, Sunday schools and companies took advantage of the serene location and the fun-filled attractions, which included boating, swimming, bowling, dancing, a rifle range, shuffleboard and baseball. Along with picnics, various groups held camps at the park as well.

Many visitors brought their own picnic lunches. However, for those who wanted something extra, they could partake of the Hotel DeKelley. This was a café known for its "ice cream and oysters" and was run by Jesse Kelley.

One of the favorite attractions occurred in early August, known as the Old Fiddlers Picnic. The picnic was the brainchild of Chris Sanderson. He and fiddlers from far and wide would gather for a day of good old country music. Initially it was known as the Chester and Delaware Counties' Old Fiddlers Picnic. The picnic moved to Hibernia County Park when Lenape Park closed in 1980.

The weather presented issues to the park being located on the Brandywine Creek. Whenever there were heavy rains, the creek would overflow and the park would be flooded. This resulted in rides being destroyed, mud flowing into the buildings and the boardwalk being ripped apart and threatened the man-made dam. But just like the Phoenix, the park would rise again to the joy of all who visited.

Due to rising costs and lower attendance, the park was sold to a local businessman in 1976. The new owner changed the name to Main Line Park. Although the name was changed, the financial status of the park did not, and the new owner put the park up for sale. In 1985, Lenape Park/Main Line Park came to an end. The beautiful hand-carved merry-go-round animals were sold, and the other rides and buildings were torn down.

WEST GROVE BOROUGH: ROSELYN THEATRE

Timeline for the Roselyn Theatre

1867 The Hall Building opens for live theater.
1915 The Hall Building is renovated and becomes the Roselyn Theatre.
1915 Heavy curtains, moving picture machine and other equipment are installed in preparation of the opening of the Roselyn.
1936 After extensive renovations and improvements, including new sound equipment and movie screen, the Roselyn plans to reopen on September 4.
1947 New seats are installed.
1980 The Roselyn Theatre is demolished.

In the center of West Grove, Pennsylvania, there is a pizza shop, an upscale restaurant, a tiny convenience store, a staffing agency and a memorial park honoring the men and women who served and gave their lives for the United States of America. Along with the granite monuments, there is a brass plaque that serves as a memorial to two buildings that provided entertainment for the community.

The Hall Building was built of brick by Joseph Pyle and opened in 1867. A general store was located on the first floor. On the second floor, there was a meeting room that became known as the Hall Building that hosted local

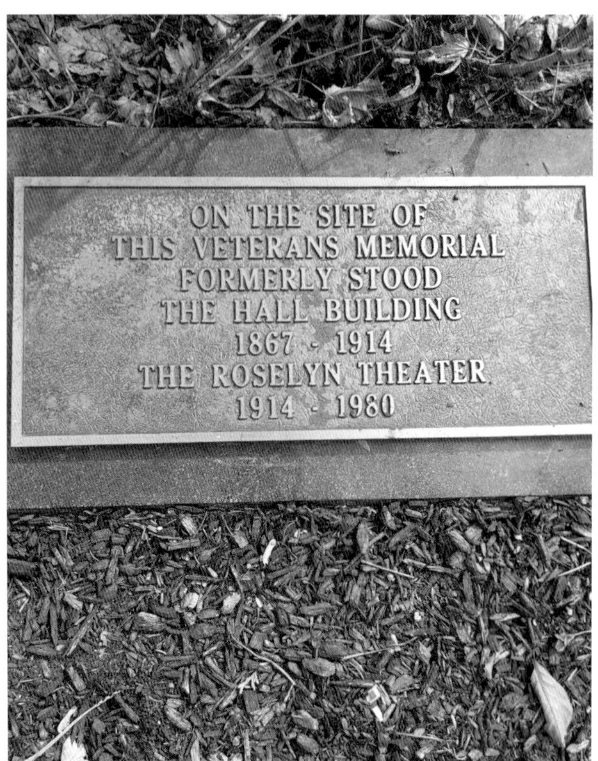

Left: On the site of the Roselyn Theatre in West Grove, there is a brass plaque that serves as a reminder of the entertainment the Roselyn provide for the residents of West Grove. *Author's collection.*

Below: The Roselyn Theatre in West Grove provided live entertainment and movies for the community for many years. *Courtesy of West Grove Historian R. Scott Steele.*

plays put on by local groups, literary society meetings with guest speakers, political meetings and debates, as well as town hall meetings. In 1914, the building needing extensive repairs. At this time, major renovations were undertaken. The old wooden structure was a fire hazard and was replaced with new steel frame construction. In 1915, the new and improved Roselyn Theatre opened.

A number of vaudeville acts played at the Roselyn Theatre, including the Guy Brothers Minstrels, 10 Big Vaudeville Acts, the Quaker City Minstrels, Enoch the Human Fish and a Sleight of Hand Ventriloquist.

Along with vaudeville acts, a number of great movies were shown. These included *Joan, the Woman* starring Geraldine Farrar; *Snow White* starring Marguerite Clark; *Davy Crockett* starring Dustin Furnum; *The Habit of Happiness*, *Reaching for the Moon*, *Headin' South* and *Mr. Fixit*, all starring Douglas Fairbanks; and *Stella Maris* and *Fanchon the Cricket*, both starring Mary Pickford.

On January 3, 1918, the Roselyn Theatre discontinued showing movies and closed the building. This was due to the war tax, lower attendance, extreme cold weather and a coal shortage. During this time, work was done on the heating system with the hope that the remodeled system would be more efficient and provide better heat.

For many years, the Roselyn Theatre provided entertainment for the community. The theater was a throwback to the days when theaters were examples of Art Deco and architectural beauty. As malls, which included modern movie theaters, began to be built in the surrounding area, local businesses began to close their doors. These included two West Grove pharmacies and a landmark all-inclusive store.

The Roselyn Theatre was abandoned and stood vacant, with broken and boarded-up windows. When it was determined that the theater would not be brought back into service, the Roselyn Theatre was demolished on September 30, 1980.

JENNERSVILLE: SUNSET PARK

As you come to the stop light on Route 796, you can turn left on to Waltman Way to go to the Avon Grove High School or right toward the Jennersville Shopping Center. Driving straight ahead, if you look on the right-hand side of the road you will see a Pennsylvania Historic Marker. What is it for? Sunset Park.

It was the height of the Depression, and money was tight for Roy Waltman, a dairy farmer who lived near West Grove, Pennsylvania. He knew that many people had come from the South seeking employment. These were people who were not interested in a northern style of music but rather longed to hear good old country music. This was a twofold solution: extra income for Roy and the right kind of music for the southern folks.

Roy had an open-air wooden stage built by local Amish craftsmen. Seating consisted of wooden planks set on cinderblocks. To add to the festive atmosphere of the place, there were carnival booths and concession stands. Realizing that not everyone would want to listen to the acts on stage, there was also bingo.

Sunset Park hosted many of the country stars who made the 750-mile drive from Nashville. These included Roy Acuff, Ernest Tubb, Lefty Frizzell, Patsy Cline, Loretta Lynn, George Jones, Johnny Cash, Dolly Parton, Tex Ritter, the Carter family, Hank Williams and Hank Williams Jr. Along with the country stars, there were also the bluegrass greats such as Bill Monroe, the Stanley brothers, Flatt & Scruggs and the Stoneman family.

Outside of the *Grand Ole Opry*, Sunset Park was one of the coveted places for new acts to play and hopefully be discovered. One such person who made his U.S. debut here was the "Singing Ranger from Nova Scotia," Hank Snow.

In the 1940s, the house band was the North Carolina Ridge Runners. Hazel Flannery played mandolin in that band. Hazel ended up marrying Lawrence Waltman, the son of founder Roy Waltman. The park provided a popular venue for fifty-five years for up-and-coming country musicians and seasoned stars to come and share their love of music with fans who traveled from all over the United States and Canada.

Sunset Park provided a unique setting for both fans and country stars. Being up close and personal, both parties co-mingled. Once a performer finished, fans would invite the star to sit with them to watch the next act.

People came from far and wide to listen to the music. One such person was twenty-one-year-old banjo player Jerry Garcia. He had listened to bluegrass records and was on a quest to learn more about that genre of music. So he jumped in his 1961 Corvair and began his cross-country trek from Palo Alto, California.

Upon arriving at Sunset Park, Jerry spent time meeting with various artists to learn more about country and bluegrass music. One person he met was David Grisman, who played the mandolin and later played on the Grateful Dead's album *American Beauty*. It would be an understatement to

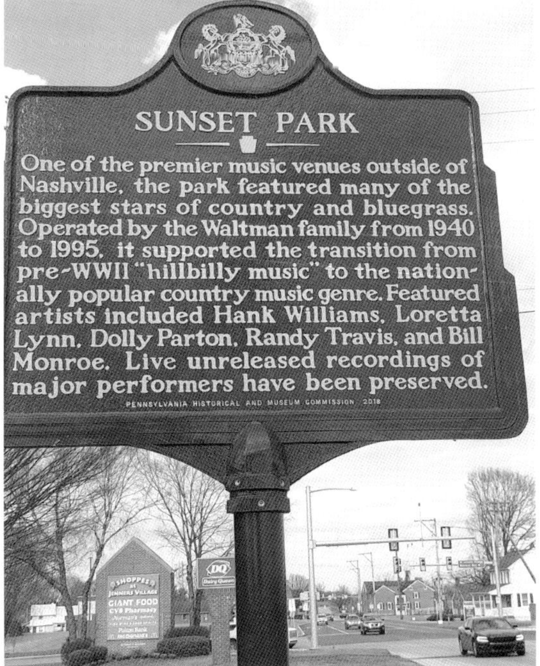

Above: Roy Waltman, known as "Uncle Roy," a dairy farmer living near West Grove, Pennsylvania, founded Sunset Park to provide much-needed extra income during the Depression. He is shown with the group the Ridge Runners. *Courtesy of West Grove Historian R. Scott Steele.*

Left: Sunset Park brought musicians from Nashville to play at this small but popular venue. Stars such as Johnny Cash, Dolly Parton and Patsy Cline played here. *Courtesy of the Pennsylvania Historical and Museum Commission.*

say that the music Garcia heard at Sunset Park influenced the music of the Grateful Dead.

Randy Travis played a show in the '80s that broke the attendance record previously set by Conway Twitty and Loretta Lynn. This was at a time when country music was making a comeback thanks to young stars such as Randy Travis.

How much impact did Sunset Park have on the music scene? The June 2017 issue of *Rolling Stone* listed the top 100 greatest country music stars. "The first five in order were Merle Haggard, Hank Williams, Johnny Cash, Loretta Lynn and the Carter Family." Sunset Park hosted these five stars multiple times.

On August 12, 2018, the Pennsylvania Historical and Museum Commission, the Penn Township Board of Supervisors and the Penn Township Historical Commission held a dedication ceremony of the historic marker for Sunset Park.

Speaking at the ceremony, then Pennsylvania senator Andrew Dinniman said:

> *Sunset Park is a great Chester County story and a great American story. It's one of a farmer and entrepreneur who had the vision to create a venue of such size, scope, and popularity that it became one of the premier places for country and bluegrass musicians to play outside of Nashville.*

A popular country music venue for fifty-five years, Sunset Park opened in 1940 and closed in 1995.

PHOENIXVILLE: THE COLONIAL THEATRE

Timeline for the Colonial Theatre

1903 Built in 1903, the Colonial is home to vaudeville acts, live stage shows and musicals.

1917 A Wurlitzer organ is installed.

1921 Coane and Pizor, new owners of the Colonial Theatre, renovate the theater, including new steps and landing and floors of concrete.

1938 A new cooling system is installed using water from a two-hundred-foot artesian well.

1949 A new motion picture screen is purchased.

1957 The Phoenix Theater Corporation purchases the Colonial Theatre.
1958 A scene in the classic science fiction movie *The Blob* is filmed locally. The Colonial Theatre is featured in pivotal scene of the movie as the creature starts to attack the town.
1958 The Colonial Theatre undergoes a complete renovation, including a large cinemascope movie screen, new seats, new carpet and new paint.
1958 On March 18, the remodeled Colonial Theatre holds its grand opening.
1975 A restored 1929 Kimball pipe organ is installed.
1996 The Colonial Theatre is scheduled to be demolished.
1996 The Association for the Colonial Theatre (ACT) is formed with a mission to restore the theater.
1996 ACT purchases the Colonial Theatre and begins restoration work.
1996 ACT develops the concept of Blobfest as a way to bring attention to Phoenixville and the Colonial Theatre.
1999 The Colonial Theatre is reopened.
1999 Blobfest, an annual three-day event each summer, begins in downtown Phoenixville, including a live reenactment of the famous scene filmed at the Colonial where screaming moviegoers flee the theater through the front doors.
2005 The Kimball organ is sold and replaced with a Wurlitzer (Opus 585) pipe organ.
2011 The old National Bank of Phoenixville building is purchased by ACT.
2016 Dedication of the Colonial Theatre and adjoining bank building.
2017 The Colonial's expanded facilities are opened for business on May 12, 2017.
2023 The Colonial is the last remaining classic theater in Phoenixville, as well as the whole of Chester County.

Built in 1903, the Colonial Opera House opened and became known for silent movies, vaudeville acts, live stage shows and musicals. Among the acts was Harry Houdini, who performed at the Colonial in 1917. Silent films were popular, and people enjoyed watching the silent movies, which were enhanced by the theater piano player. In 1928, the first talking film, *The Jazz Singer*, premiered at the Colonial.

The Blob was filmed in its entirety by Good News Productions, located in Yellow Springs, except for two scenes: the classic run-out scene at the

Colonial and the Downingtown Diner scene. There is a commemorative plaque on the rear wall of the balcony inside the Colonial that reads:

> *Through this wall in the year 1958, Shorty Yeaworth's* The Blob *brought the monster into the movie theater and Phoenixville's* Colonial Theatre *into the annals of film history.*

Blobfest is a three-day event held every summer. Along with other horror movies, *The Blob* is shown repeatedly. There is also "a film competition, scream contest, street fair, and live entertainment." The highlight of the weekend is the reenactment of the iconic run-out scene, where excited *Blob* fans get to participate in the action.

Once again, this is an example of what happens when concerned citizens rally together to preserve a piece of history. The fact that the Colonial Theatre is the last remaining classic theater in Phoenixville and all of Chester County shows what can happen when people do not allow historic structures to decay and disappear or simply be demolished.

WEST PIKELAND TOWNSHIP: GOOD NEWS PRODUCTIONS

Irvin Shortness "Shorty" Yeaworth Jr. was the son of a Presbyterian minister. Shorty did go to seminary; however, he came to the conclusion that everyone has different gifts and callings and that preaching the gospel inside a church building was not his calling.

Instead, he chose to take up filmmaking, which from an early age was something that fascinated him and was something he wished to pursue. Moving away from the traditional method of delivering the gospel message, Shorty decided that he was better suited to present the Christian message through the lens of a camera.

Believing that he was to use film as a primary way to deliver the gospel, Shorty became the premier film producer of Christian films during his career. In order to bring this goal to life, in 1952 Shorty purchased the village of Yellow Springs, which became home to Good News Productions.

The various buildings of Yellow Springs were transformed into apartments and dormitories for staff, kitchen facilities where crew took turns cooking and serving, studios for filming, an editing facility and administrative offices.

There is an informational plaque at Chester Springs for Good News Production. *Author's collection.*

There was a staff of about fifty people according to Craig Swain; these included "production managers, scriptwriters, sound recorders, photographers, animators, cameramen, lighting technicians, and actors… [also] assistant directors, prop men, makeup men, and press people."

Good News Productions ran from 1952 until 1973. During its twenty-two years at Yellow Springs, more than four hundred films were made, along with a number of radio and television shows. Two films that became well known, although most people do not know that Good News Productions produced them, were *4D Man* and *The Blob*.

The Christian films and Christian TV shows Good News produced were not the same as a blockbuster film that would be shown in theaters throughout the country. While wondering how his could happen, Shorty happened upon a gooey material produced by Union Carbide. The creative minds of Good News Productions came together, and *The Blob* came into being.

All the scenes for *The Blob* were filmed at Yellow Springs except for several location shots. The first was the classic run-out scene, filmed at the Colonial Theatre in Phoenixville, Pennsylvania. Here moviegoers come running and screaming out of the theater because the Blob is oozing into the theater. A second scene was filmed at a diner in Downingtown, Pennsylvania. The scenes at the doctor's house were filmed at a doctor's house in Phoenixville, as were the school shots at the local junior high school. Once the editing was complete on *The Blob*, the movie was sold to Paramount Pictures, which released it nationally in 1958.

Two actors and two songwriters got their start in the film industry through Good News Productions. Steve McQueen, unknown at the time, had his first major film start with *The Blob*. Prior to becoming a well-known actress, the eleven- or twelve-year-old Patty Duke appeared in *4D Man*. Relatively unknown at the time, Burt Bacharach and Hal David were hired by Paramount Pictures to write the theme song for *The Blob*.

Shorty Yeaworth directing Steve McQueen during a scene from *The Blob*. *Courtesy of the Vince Spangler Collection, Historic Yellow Springs Moore Archives.*

Shorty Yeaworth felt that it was a life's mission to help young people learn filmmaking not from sitting in lectures in college but rather through hands-on experience. Students were able to be a part of producing a film from the creative process of developing a theme and script all the way to filming, editing and promoting the film. Good News Productions was a microcosm of the Hollywood experience. Being in such an intimate setting, the film stars were part of the family and helped cook, clean and relax.

It was an amazing twenty-two years for all those who had the privilege of being part of Good News Productions. Due to limited financial success and the fire that destroyed his editing facility, Shorty made the decision to put Yellow Springs up for sale in 1973.

Shorty left Yellow Springs and continued his artistic endeavors by producing various shows, making films, doing set design and developing theme parks. Shorty was on assignment in Jordan when an automobile accident resulted in his death in 2004.

OXFORD: WHEELER'S CIRCUS

Driving toward Oxford from West Grove, Pennsylvania, you pass the Flowers Food Bakery, which makes Nature's Own bread products. A short distance after Flowers Foods is the apartment complex known as Oxhaven Apartments. This used to be the site of fairgrounds developed by the Oxford Agricultural Society (OAS).

The OAS purchased land in Oxford in 1870 to set up a fairground. Beginning that year, a fall fair/festival was held on an annual basis. The fair was held to promote agriculture and agricultural products from the surrounding area. Farmers proudly displayed their livestock, children displayed their vegetables and women showed their weaving and needlepoint. This event attracted up to twelve thousand attendees.

On those fairgrounds, a local circus spent its winters there. The founder of the circus was a man named Alson Wheeler. Wheeler became involved with the circus industry at the age of nineteen. In 1893, Wheeler created his first circus. It was a one-ring wagon circus.

In the winter of 1906, Wheeler and his circus came to Oxford for the first time. By now, he had changed the name to Wheeler's New Model Shows. It was still a one-ring circus. In the winter months, while repairs were being made to the wagons and the circus crew were practicing new acts, Wheeler leased the Oxford Opera House and ran movies along with shows. In April

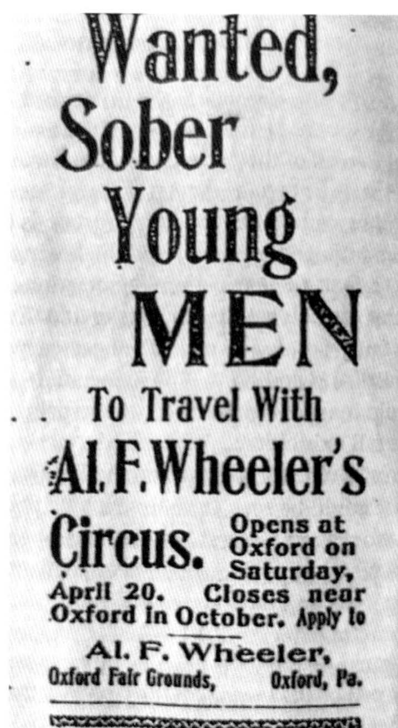

Left: Advertisement for workers need for the Wheeler Circus. *Courtesy of the Oxford Area Historical Association.*

Right: In April 1909, Mr. Wheeler had a two-ring circus that was the largest circus east of the Mississippi. *Courtesy of the Oxford Area Historical Association.*

1907, the New Model Show opened at the Oxford Agricultural Society Fairgrounds. Wheeler advertised for local help to join his circus.

It was an exciting time for both adults and children during the winter months because they got to view the circus animals. According to Gail Roberts's "The Wheeler Circus," these included "a boa constrictor, elephants, bears, hyenas, a giraffe, zebras, and leopards."

April 1909 brought about the Wheeler two-ring circus. The citizens of Oxford were fortunate because they were the first ones to view the new circus, which was the largest circus east of the Mississippi.

Wheeler was constantly looking to expand. New wagons, new animals and new employees were added. By 1910, Wheeler's wagon show was considered one of the largest in the country. Also in 1910, Wheeler signed a five-year lease with the Oxford Agricultural Society to utilize the fairgrounds during the winter months.

With the railroad becoming more popular, in 1911 Wheeler began transporting his circus on the railroad. Unfortunately, the Oxford railroad station could not accommodate all of Wheelers circus train cars, so the decision was made to move his circus to Georgia for the winter months.

Not wanting to miss out on needed income, the railroad siding in Oxford was expanded in order to accommodate all of Wheeler's train cars. At this time, the circus grew to three rings.

Wheeler was doing well financially, and in 1913, he decided to purchase the Oxford Fairgrounds from the Oxford Agricultural Association, formerly known as the Oxford Agricultural Society. The circus continued to grow, and in 1914, former Ringling Bros. circus acts joined the Wheeler circus.

Ever the entrepreneur and looking for a way to increase his financial standing, Wheeler began to sell housing lots from the fairgrounds land in 1919. This continued for almost ten years, while he remained active in the circus business.

Wheeler worked with the Ringling Bros. Circus. In 1928, Wheeler worked with the Sylvan-Drew Circus. Finding out that the Sylvan-Drew Circus was having financial challenges, Wheeler decided to purchase the circus in 1930. The circus was renamed the Al. F. Wheeler Circus. It was also known as the New Model Shows. The circus was brought to Oxford in the spring. His final circus venture was the Wheeler and Almond Circus, which he brought to Oxford in May 1933.

Upon his retirement from the circus industry, Wheeler focused on his real estate business. Having brought jobs and entertainment to Oxford, and having helped the railroad grow in Oxford, Wheeler passed away in May 1957. Not many people can say that they had an actual circus stay in their town.

Chapter 7
UNDERGROUND RAILROAD

KENNETT SQUARE: LONGWOOD PROGRESSIVE FRIENDS MEETINGHOUSE AND CEMETERY

Longwood Gardens, located near the borough of Kennett Square, Pennsylvania, is one of the great gardens of the world and the most visited garden in America. Each year, more than 1 million visitors enjoy the botanical marvel. And every year, those visitors on their way in and their way out drive past a tall white building that has a sign over the entranceway reading "Brandywine Valley Tourism Information."

Visitors must wonder if this tall white building was created simply to house a tourism information center. Can this be? Indeed not. Instead, this building, the Longwood Progressive Friends Meetinghouse, is an important part of Chester County history.

Before the issue of slavery and emancipation became a national issue, the Society of Friends (also known as Quakers) in 1776 decided that owning slaves was no longer compatible with the teachings of the Quakers and that if a Quaker chose to continue owning slaves, that person would no longer be a part of the Quaker community.

The idea of forming the Pennsylvania Yearly Meeting of Progressive Friends, also known as the Longwood Progressive Friends Meeting (LPFM), came about in 1853 due to the division among local Quakers on the issue of slavery and other reform issues of the day. The LPFM believed that action needed to be taken, including promoting the cause of abolition and being involved with the Underground Railroad.

A series of events furthered the growing division between the conservative and progressive Quakers, ending in the founding of LPFM. This included progressive Quakers being disowned by their home meeting due to their "worldly activities," including speaking out against slavery, speaking in favor of the abolishment of slavery and participating in the Underground Railroad.

Finally, it was decided to hold a conference on May 22, 1853, at the Old Kennett Meetinghouse to discuss establishing their own meeting. Fifty-eight men and women attended the conference, and the Pennsylvania Yearly Meeting of Progressive Friends was founded. John and Hannah (née Peirce) Cox, having been dismissed from the Old Kennett Friends Meeting, were not only founding members of the LPFM. They also sold a parcel of their Longwood Farm on which a meetinghouse would be built.

The Longwood Progressive Friends Meetinghouse was home to abolitionists, many who were Quakers, who believed that actions, not words, were needed to end slavery. *Courtesy of the Chester County History Center.*

Above: Today, the Longwood Progressive Friends Meetinghouse is home to the Brandywine Valley Tourism Information Center. *Author's collection.*

Left: The Harriet Tubman Underground Railroad Byway begins in Maryland. One of the destinations is the Longwood Progressive Friends Meetinghouse. *Author's collection.*

On September 3, 1854, the cornerstone was laid, and the building was dedicated on May 19, 1855.

Many of the fifty-eight founders lived in the proximity of the new meetinghouse. These included Eusebius Barnard, John and Hannah Cox and Dr. Bartholomew Fussell. LPFM and its members played a major role in the abolitionist movement, the antislavery movement and the workings of the Underground Railroad. Thomas Garrett and his assistants helped more than two thousand freedom seekers, as did Dr. Bartholomew Fussell.

LPFM was host to many abolitionist speakers, including Sojourner Truth, Frederick Douglass, Harriet Beecher Stowe, William Lloyd Garrison and John Greenleaf Whittier.

After the Civil War, emancipation and the abolishment of slavery, the meeting continued until 1940, when it was discontinued and Pierre S. DuPont (owner of Longwood Gardens) purchased the property. The building was used for a variety of purposes and currently is leased to the Chester County Conference and Visitors Bureau, which set up the Brandywine Valley Tourism Information Center.

The Longwood Progressive Friends Meetinghouse and Cemetery have been placed in the National Register of Historic Places and designated a National Park Service Network to Freedom Site. The meetinghouse and cemetery are also a designated stop on the Harriett Tubman Underground Railroad Byway.

This tall white building stands as a lasting legacy to the members and the influence they had both locally and nationally that brought about the signing of the Emancipation Proclamation by President Abraham Lincoln and the fulfillment of their abolitionist activities.

KENNETT SQUARE: PRESIDENT LINCOLN AND THE LONGWOOD PROGRESSIVE FRIENDS MEETING

Conservative Quakers believed that simply not owning slaves was enough. The Pennsylvania Yearly Meeting of Progressive Friends, also known as the Longwood Progressive Friends Meeting (LPFM), was founded by progressive Quakers, abolitionists and other like-minded people who firmly believed that actions, not words, were needed to end slavery, including being active in the Underground Railroad and the abolitionist movement.

With that belief in mind, LPFM members actively lobbied for the emancipation of enslaved people. On June 20, 1862, three men and three women met with President Abraham Lincoln and presented him with a "memorial" or petition. Three members of the delegation—William Barnard, Thomas Garrett and Dinah Mendenhall—were active in the Underground Railroad. William Barnard was Lincoln's third cousin once removed (although at the time of this meeting neither man knew this). Five members of the delegation were founding members of the Longwood Progressive Friends Meeting: William Barnard, Thomas Garrett, Dinah Mendenhall, Oliver Johnson and Alice Hambleton. Eliza Agnew was the sixth member.

The LPFM delegation was warmly received by President Lincoln. Unlike the Philadelphia Yearly Meeting, which opposed war in any form, the progressive Quakers understood the dilemma Lincoln faced (going to war to keep the Union intact) and empathized with him on the situation.

With that said, the LPFM delegation emphasized its desire to the president to see all enslaved people emancipated. Understanding the concept of "Inner Light," the president told the delegation that he needed "Divine assistance" to guide him in making the best decision possible.

Because of their dedication to the cause of the abolition of slavery and the emancipation of enslaved people, the LPFM was successful in presenting its passionate request to President Lincoln and seeing the desired results come to fruition. A little over a month from the LPFM delegation meeting with Lincoln, on July 22, Lincoln presented the rough draft of the Emancipation Proclamation with his cabinet. The president issued the Emancipation Proclamation in September 1862, and it took effect on January 1, 1863.

The memorial that the six members of LPFM brought to President Lincoln was reprinted in the *Bulletin for the 150th Anniversary Celebration of Longwood Progressive Friends Meetinghouse*, held on May 22, 2005. It reads as follows:

> *Memorial to the President*
> *To Abraham Lincoln, President of the United States,*
> *The Religious Society of Friends, in Yearly Meeting assembled at Longwood, Chester County, from the 5th to 7th of the sixth month, 1862, under a solemn sense of the perils besetting the country, and the duty of devolving upon them to exert whatever influence they possess to rescue it from the impending destruction, beg leave respectfully but earnestly, to set forth the consideration of President Lincoln—That they fully share in the general grief and reprobation felt at the seditious course pursued in opposition to the General Government by the so-called "Confederate States" regarding it as marked by all the revolting features of high-handed robbery, cruel*

treachery, and murderous violence, and therefore utterly to the abhorrent and condemned by every over of his country and every friend of the human race.

That, nevertheless, this sanguinary rebellion finds its cause, purpose, and combustible materials in that most unchristian and barbarous system of slavery which prevails in that section of the country and in the guilt of which the whole land has long been deeply involved by general complicity, so that it is tobe contritely recognized as the penalty due to such persistent, flagrant trans-gressions, and as the inevitable operation of the law of eternal justice.

That thus heavily visited for it grinding oppression of an unfortunate race, "peeled, meted out, and trodden under foot" whose wrongs have so long cried unto heaven for redress, and thus solemnly warned of the infatuation as well as exceeding wickedness of endeavoring to secure peace, prosperity, and unity, while leaving millions to clank their chains in the house of bondage, the nations, in its official organization should lose no time proclaiming immediate and universal emancipation, so that the present frightful effusion of blood may cease, liberty be established, and permanent reconciliation effected by the removal of the sole cause of these divisions.

That in his speech delivered in Springfield, before his election to the Office of Chief Magistrate, the President expressly declared, "a house divided against itself cannot stand. I believe this government cannot endure permanently half slave and half free. I do not expect the Union to be dissolved—I do not expect the house to fall—but I do expect it will cease to be divided. It will become all one thing, or all the other." That this society, therefore, urgently unites with a widespread and constant increasing sentiment in beseeching the President, as the head of the nation, clothed with the constitutional power in such a fearful emergency, to suppress the rebellion effectually by the removal of its cause, not to allow the present golden opportunity to pass without decreeing the entire abolition of slavery throughout the land, as a measure imperatively demanded by a due respect for the unity of the country, the safety and happiness of the people, the preservation of free institutions, and by every consideration of justice, mercy, and peace. Otherwise, we have fearful reason to apprehend that blood will continue to flow and fierce dissensions to abound, and calamities increase, and fiery judgements to be poured out, until the work of national destruction is consummated beyond hope of recovery.

KENNETT SQUARE: THE COX HOUSE

When you leave Longwood Gardens outside of Kennett Square, Pennsylvania, and turn right on Route 1, you continue a short distance when you see a boarded-up (actually mothballed) white-washed house on the right-hand side of Route 1. Who lived there, and why is the house still standing?

John and Hannah (née Peirce) Cox were staunch abolitionists, active with Underground Railroad (UGRR), and were founding members of the Longwood Progressive Friends Meeting. The home they lived in, Longwood, was Hannah's childhood home. Longwood became a major stop on the UGRR for freedom seekers coming from Delaware.

The Delaware/Pennsylvania border was four miles from Longwood and ten miles from the Wilmington, Delaware home of Thomas Garrett, another abolitionist and active Underground Railroad member who worked closely with John and Hannah Cox.

Thomas Garrett hired free blacks to help transport freedom seekers northward. One man, Jackson, often brought the freedom seekers to the Cox house, often in the middle of the night. Jackson would knock on the fence and announce the arrivals of "Friends." Freedom seekers came from Delaware, Maryland, Virginia and North Carolina. During their journey to freedom, if they came to the Line House on Route 52 (the Delaware-Pennsylvania border), they knew that they were entering into a free state.

The freedom seekers were hidden in the attic of the Cox home. If word was brought that slave catchers were on the way, the freedom seekers would be sent out into the fields and woods and sent to the next UGRR station. The home had a widow's walk where a lookout would keep a watchful eye for slave catchers and freedom seekers.

John and Hannah would gladly feed the freedom seekers and provide clothing as needed. Once rested, the freedom seekers were loaded into a wagon and taken to the next stop on the UGRR. Because the house was so close to the Delaware-Pennsylvania border, freedom seekers were moved farther north to the next UGRR station.

John and Hannah Cox believed that each human being was a child of God and should be treated with dignity and respect. That is why over the years working with the Underground Railroad, they willingly risked their lives and fortune to provide shelter, food and comfort for freedom seekers. Their house, being a major stop on the Underground Railroad, helped just some of the estimated fifty thousand freedom seekers who passed through Chester County on their journey to freedom. The Cox house was purchased

The boundary between Delaware and Pennsylvania runs through the Line House. Freedom-seeking enslaved people knew that they were free when they went past this house. *Author's collection.*

Above: The Cox House, Longwood Farm, provided shelter in the basement and the attic. A tunnel in the basement was used by freedom-seeking enslaved people to escape. *Courtesy of the Chester County History Center.*

Left: The Cox House, Longwood Farm, is owned by Longwood Gardens and is presently awaiting funding to begin restoration of this historic structure. *Author's collection.*

Did You Know?

The Names Kennett Square Is Known For

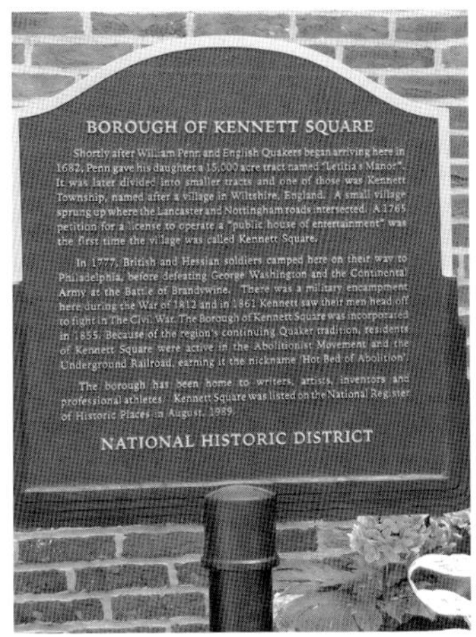

Kennett Square, Pennsylvania, was known as the hotbed of abolition and had more Underground Railroad stations in the Kennett area than anywhere else. *Author's collection.*

Kennett Square produces 65 percent of the mushrooms consumed in the United States, and Kennett Square mushrooms are the largest cash crop in Pennsylvania. This is why Kennett Square is known as the "mushroom capital of the world." Prior to this, Kennett Square was known by two other names.

The first was the "hotbed of abolitionism." Kennett Square was home to many progressive Quakers, who were staunch abolitionists who championed the emancipation of enslaved people. Kennett Square was also home to the Kennett Square Anti-Slavery Society and often hosted the meetings of the Pennsylvania Anti-Slavery Society.

The second was the "hub of the Underground Railroad." There were more Underground Railroad stations in the Kennett Square area than anywhere else.

by Longwood Gardens. Hopefully sometime in the future the home will be restored and opened to the public as a testament to John and Hannah Cox and their dedication to seeing enslaved people become free either via the Underground Railroad or by the abolition of slavery.

UPPER OXFORD TOWNSHIP: HOSANNA CHURCH

The only remaining building left from the town of Hinsonville is the Hosanna Church. Hinsonville residents held worship services in various homes for a number of year. In 1843, a decision was made to move from home worship services to a building of worship.

The men who help found Hinsonville also helped build Hosanna. These included the three Wall brothers, the three Amos brothers, Samuel Glasgow and Emory Hinson. Funds were raised, and in 1845 a little brick church was dedicated. The building held about one hundred worshipers.

Hosanna was one of the earliest Black churches located in Chester County. The church established a cemetery that turned out to be one of the first Black cemeteries to put the names of the deceased African Americans on the headstones. Some of the tombstones bear the original African names of church members.

Hosanna also played a role in the Underground Railroad in Chester County as one of the station stops. Being a community of African Americans, it wanted to assist freedom seekers any way possible on their journey to freedom. Freedom seekers traveling from Virginia and Maryland would stop at Hosanna and be given food and clothing to change into.

Enslaved people were given off Saturday noon until Sunday evening. Enslaved people coming for the worship service would mingle with the free blacks. If the master had not yet come back to pick them up, they often would get on a carriage or wagon and be driven to a nearby Underground Railroad station.

Frederick Douglass offered high praise for Hosanna and the work it did for the sake of freedom seekers. Hosanna Church was one of the stops for Harriet Tubman as she escorted freedom seekers north from Maryland and Virginia.

A variety of speakers came to Hosanna to speak about the Underground Railroad, the emancipation of enslaved people and the abolition of slavery. Speakers included Frederick Douglass, Harriet Tubman and Sojourner Truth.

The inside of the church still has the original pulpit and the chairs where the pastor and elders would sit. A furnace and bathroom were added later. The pews are original.

There is a rich history when it comes to Hosanna Church. The church was the center of the community of Hinsonville, it provided opportunities for aspiring preachers to hone their skills, it opened its doors to abolitionist and antislavery speakers and it played a pivotal role in the Underground Railroad helping freedom seekers on their journey to freedom.

Today, the church stands vacant and in need of much repair. Hopefully, in the near future Hosanna Church can be restored to its former glory and reflect the legacy and history that developed over its years in existence.

Above: After meeting in each other's homes for Sunday service, the residents of Hinsonville decided to build their own church and meetinghouse: Hosanna Church. *Author's collection.*

Opposite: Hosanna Church played a significant role in the lives of those freedom-seeking enslaved people on their journey to freedom. *Courtesy of the Pennsylvania Historical and Museum Commission.*

An inside view of the Hosanna Church, which played an important role in the Underground Railroad. *Author's collection.*

WEST CHESTER: LAST SPEECH OF FREDERICK DOUGLASS

Frederick Douglass was born into slavery in February 1818 near Easton, Maryland. He was raised by his grandparents until he was six years old. At that time, his grandmother dropped him off at the master's plantation and left.

Two years later, the master sent Frederick to relatives in Baltimore, where he was a houseboy. The lady of the house began to teach him to read; however, when her husband found out, he put a stop to that. Wanting to continue to learn, Frederick exchanged his food with local boys who taught him the basics of reading and writing.

Frederick returned to the plantation when he was about fifteen and learned firsthand the unbelievable conditions slaves had to endure. After a failed attempt to escape, he was sent back to Baltimore to live with his master's relatives once again. The second attempt at escaping was successful.

Moving north, he attended abolitionist and antislavery meetings, where he met William Lloyd Garrison, a well-known abolitionist. This was the beginning of his career of speaking out against slavery and the need to emancipate all enslaved people.

Douglass was acknowledged as a passionate and committed abolitionist. In his speeches, he championed the downtrodden and the less fortunate. A staunch believer in equal rights and justice for all, he was not only antislavery but also supported women's rights.

Douglass spoke at many places in Chester County, including the Longwood Progressive Friends Meetinghouse, Hosanna Church and the Oxford Clarkson Anti-Slavery Society.

Douglass gave many speeches at West Chester University. His last speech at West Chester was on February 1, 1895. In his speech, Douglass stressed that slavery was an experiment and that freedom is the norm. He spoke out against and denounced the activities that were occurring against Black people, including lynchings and murders. He hoped that reform would take place and that the life of the Black person would improve.

Frederick Douglass visited West Chester University often. On February 1, 1895, Douglass gave his last speech at the university. He hoped that reform would take place and that Black people's lives would improve. *Courtesy of the Pennsylvania Historical and Museum Commission.*

Douglass stressed that African Americans are American citizens, and as such, they deserved the same treatment as other American citizens. He believed that they should be treated as fairly as the immigrants coming to the shores of America. He declared, "African-Americans are friends of America—all they want is a fair chance."

Frederick Douglass died on February 20, 1895—just nineteen days after his speech at West Chester University. The Pennsylvania Historic Marker for Douglass was dedicated on February 1, 2006—the 111th anniversary of Douglass's last speech at West Chester University.

EMBREEVILLE: THE STARGAZER STONE

Both William Penn and Lord Calvert received land in the New World from the Crown. One day, a sea captain came to William Penn and informed him that Philadelphia was actually located in the colony of Maryland. Being the only major seaport for Pennsylvania, this was unacceptable to William Penn.

Penn and Calvert hired local surveyors to try to resolve the issue, but neither man was happy with the results. They reached out to the Royal Observatory in London to see who it might recommend to come and survey the boundary lines between Pennsylvania and Maryland. In 1763, Jeremiah Dixon and Charles Mason arrived in Philadelphia to begin their work.

Their first order of business was to survey the location of Philadelphia, which they determined was actually part of Pennsylvania. They went on to survey the rest of the boundary lines. One thing needed was a reference point to verify their survey findings. On January 7, 1764, Mason and Dixon found the site they were searching for. It was located on the Joel Harlan Farm in Embreeville, Pennsylvania.

They marked the site with a large quartz rock secured in the ground over which a tripod was placed to take celestial readings. The main point of reference was Polaris, or the North Star. This is the same star, years later, that enslaved people used to chart their course northward to freedom.

Farmers riding by on horse or in their wagons watched Mason set his tripod over the quartz stone and gaze toward the heavens. The farmers appropriately nicknamed the stone the "Stargazer Stone."

Up until the Mason-Dixon line, most state boundaries were mapped out according to rivers and mountain chains. This boundary was different in that it was "man-made," determined by surveying an arbitrary line.

The Mason-Dixon line became the boundary line that could make the difference between freedom and liberty and a life of misery and hopelessness. *Courtesy of the Pennsylvania Historical and Museum Commission.*

On September 11, 1768, Mason and Dixon completed their work and left for England. This was the last time they worked together as a survey team.

The survey work of Mason and Dixon was formally approved on November 9, 1768. Thus ended an eighty-seven-year land disagreement between the Penn and Calvert families. In an ironic twist of fate, the land the two parties finally agreed on would, after the American Revolution, become part of the newly created United States of America.

When Mason and Dixon left America, the boundary they had surveyed had not been named. The land dispute had been settled, and the boundary was looked on simply as a dividing line between the colonies of Maryland and Pennsylvania—no more, no less.

That all changed on March 1, 1780, when the Assembly of Pennsylvania passed the Gradual Emancipation Act—the first such act passed by any state in the Union. With that one piece of legislation, the long-forgotten boundary between Pennsylvania and Maryland suddenly became the difference between freedom and slavery for many enslaved people. The names of Mason and Dixon were resurrected, and the "Mason-Dixon line" became widely known.

Freedom seekers began heading in earnest toward the free state of Pennsylvania, traveling north from Virginia and Maryland. Just as Mason and Dixon depended on the North Star to verify their survey results, freedom seekers likewise depended on the North Star to guide them north to freedom.

As Mason and Dixon completed sections of the boundary, they would place boundary stones every mile and a Crown stone every five miles. The boundary stones had an "M" on one side and a "P" on the other—Maryland and Pennsylvania. If the sky were overcast and the North Star was not able to be seen, freedom seekers could crawl along; if they came in contact with a stone, they could feel for the "P" and know that was the right direction.

In 1908, Henry (great-grandson of Joel) and Elizabeth Harlan donated the Stargazer Stone and a section of land to the Chester County Historical Society. To better protect this historic piece of quartz, the society had a stone

This white quartz stone was named the "Stargazer Stone" by farmers who would watch Mason and Dixon reference it when making accurate celestial readings. *Author's collection.*

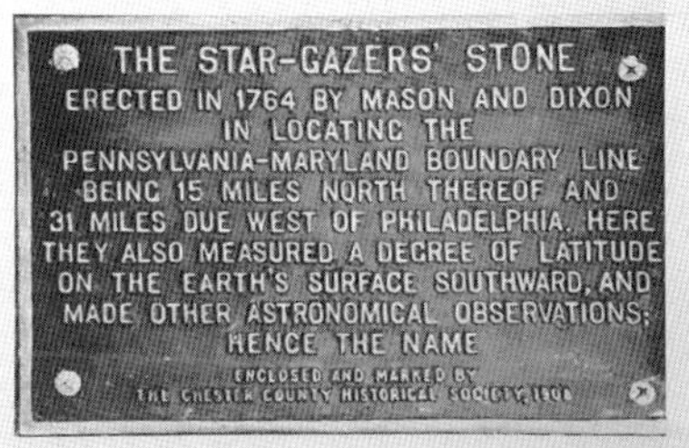

Left: In 1908, the Chester County Historical Society built a stone wall around the Stargazer Stone to protect it. *Author's collection.*

Above: To memorialize the Harlan descendants deeding the Stargazer Stone to the Chester County Historical Society, the society placed a plaque on the stone wall it built. *Author's collection.*

wall built around the stone, as well as mounted a historic plaque on one of the larger stones. The society turned the site over to Chester County.

The Stargazer Stone is listed in the National Register of Historical Places. The Stargazer Stone has also been designated a National Civil Engineering Landmark. This is only one of 125 such sites in the United States. This historic landmark can be visited by going to Stargazers' Stone Park, 899 Stargazer Road, Embreeville, Pennsylvania, 19382.

Chapter 8

WOMEN'S SUFFRAGE

WEST CHESTER/VALLEY FORGE: THE JUSTICE BELL

Sixty-three years after the first women's rights convention was held in West Chester, Chester County, suffragist and activist Katharine Wentworth Ruschenberger of Chester County was trying to figure out a way to promote women's voting rights.

Living close to Philadelphia, Katharine she knew about the Liberty Bell—one of the most well-known symbols of freedom and independence. That is when the Justice Bell, also known as the Women's Liberty Bell and the Suffrage Bell, was born.

Katharine hired the Meneely Bell Foundry in Troy, New York, to produce the bell. It was similar to the Liberty Bell except for two major differences—there was no crack and the words "Establish JUSTICE" were added. On the Justice Bell, the following was written:

Establish JUSTICE
Proclaim LIBERTY throughout all the Land unto
All the inhabitants Thereof
Meneeley Bell Co
Troy, NY
MCMXV

Chester County resident Mrs. Ruschenberger and her Justice Bell, which she took on tour throughout Pennsylvania to promote women's suffrage. *Courtesy of the Chester County History Center.*

Now that Katharine had her Justice Bell, she bought a flatbed truck on which the bell was mounted. The bell clapper was chained so the bell could not ring. This was done to emphasize that women were silenced and did not have the right to vote. Along with the bell, there was a sign proclaiming the suffragist movement's slogan "Votes for Women."

In 1915, the Justice Bell was taken on a five-thousand-mile tour of the sixty-seven Pennsylvania counties in order to promote women's suffrage. Leaflets were handed out during the tour that read:

> *The Women's Liberty Bell—"Liberty throughout the land to all the inhabitants thereof" was the message of the Liberty Bell of 1776. It proclaimed the birth of a new nation "DEDICATED TO THE PROPOSITION THE GOVERNMENTS DERIVE THEIR POWER FROM THE CONSENT OF THE GOVERNED" AND THAT "TAXATION WITHOUT REPRESENTATION IS TYRNNY* [sic]." *Today, fifty million of these inhabitants are women...The new bell is the Women's Liberty Bell, which is to ring for the first time on the day that Women of Pennsylvania are granted the right to vote...The*

> *Liberty Bell 1776 rang to "Proclaim Liberty" to create our nation. "The Womens' Liberty Bell" will ring to establish justice to complete our nation. Help break the chains that hold the bronze clapper silent. Vote "Yes" on the Suffrage Amendment on Election Day Pennsylvania.*

In spite of their efforts, the Pennsylvania referendum on women's right to vote failed in 1915. Chester County was one of the counties to vote in favor of the right for women to vote. The Nineteenth Amendment, giving women the right to vote, went up for ratification in 1920. So once again the Justice Bell went on tour—not only in Pennsylvania but in other states as well. The Congressional Union for Women Suffrage held a convention in Washington, D.C., and the Justice Bell was there.

On August 18, 1920, the Nineteenth Amendment was ratified. Katharine Wentworth Ruschenberger rang the Justice Bell during a ceremony held at Independence Hall in Philadelphia, Pennsylvania. The bell was rung forty-eight times for the then forty-eight states in the Union. Just a short two years later in 1922, Martha Thomas, a Chester County resident and suffragette, was elected to the Pennsylvania legislature—the first woman to be elected.

After the passage of the Nineteenth Amendment, the Justice Bell was no longer needed, and it resided in Mrs. Rushenberger's backyard. Upon her death in 1943, the bell was, per her will, given to the Washington Memorial Chapel. For fifty years, it lay in the woods abandoned and forgotten.

In 1992, a new rector was installed at the church. He discovered the historic bell and rallied the Daughters of the American Revolution and the Pennsylvania League of Voters to fundraise. With the monies raised, the Justice Bell was placed in the National Patriots Bell Tower, located at the Washington Memorial Chapel, where it is on public display.

The Justice Bell has only left the chapel once. In April 1995, to honor the seventy-fifth anniversary of the League of Women's Voters, the bell was first displayed in Harrisburg at the State Museum of Pennsylvania. After that, the Justice Bell traveled throughout Pennsylvania for a year prior to returning to its permanent location at the Washington Memorial Chapel.

WEST CHESTER: WOMEN'S RIGHTS CONVENTION OF 1852

The women's rights movement was started in 1848 when a group of women met in Seneca Falls, New York. A national movement had begun, and additional conventions were held in New York, Ohio and Massachusetts.

The seventh convention, and first for Pennsylvania, was held in West Chester, Chester County, from June 2 to June 3, 1852. West Chester was chosen as the host due to the number of women abolitionists and women's rights advocates living in Chester County. A letter read at the beginning of the convention stated, "In no part of the State could a community be found better qualified to appreciate the objects of such a meeting…Chester [County] has undoubtedly taken the lead of all her sister Counties in Educational movements."

The West Chester Convention was organized by Hannah Darlington. Hannah was a founding member of the Longwood Progressive Friends Meeting. She and her husband, Chandler, were Quakers and staunch abolitionists and were active in the Underground Railroad.

The main speech was given by Dr. Ann Preston, a Quaker and abolitionist and whose house was an active station on the Underground Railroad. Her father, Amos Preston, was a founding member of the Longwood Progressive Friends Meeting. She had recently graduated from the first class of the Female Medical College of Philadelphia. Her uncle, Dr. Bartholomew Fussell, an abolitionist and active member of the Underground Railroad, sat on the board of the Female Medical College of Philadelphia.

The first women's rights convention in Pennsylvania was held in West Chester, which was chosen as the host due to the number of women abolitionists and women's rights advocates living in Chester County. *Courtesy of the Pennsylvania Historical and Museum Commission.*

As such, she knew firsthand what it was like to experience opposition from a typically male-dominated profession. In her speech, she advocated for the right of women to pursue education and any career they chose. Dr. Harriot Hunt traveled from Boston to address the convention. Unable to attend, Dr. Elizabeth Blackwell, who was the first woman to graduate from medical school, sent a congratulatory message.

At the end of the convention, the attendees approved a variety of resolutions. Among them, the women wanted the freedom to study medicine and other related subjects. Chester County was home to many Quakers. The Quaker concept that all human beings are created equal became a rallying cry of the women activists.

Other well-known attendees at the time included Lucretia Mott (a Quaker abolitionist), Ernestine Rose (promoter of women's rights and an abolitionist) and Frances D. Gage (active in the antislavery movement and women's rights). Many of the early supporters of women's rights were men. One of them was a twenty-four-year-old young man named Evan Pugh. He had the opportunity to deliver a short speech in which he said, "The question of women's rights affects the whole human race. We know from sad experience that man cannot rise while woman is degraded."

Chapter 9

WARTIME IN CHESTER COUNTY

WEST PIKELAND TOWNSHIP: YELLOW SPRINGS REVOLUTIONARY WAR HOSPITAL

The Revolutionary War battles resulted in more than one thousand Continental soldiers being killed or wounded every year of the war. Due to the lack of understanding of germs and how diseases spread, the number of deaths from disease outnumbered battle deaths nine to one.

Soldiers came from throughout the colonies, and with them they brought a variety of diseases, including typhus, smallpox, tuberculosis and the flu. As the men lived in cramped and germ-infested conditions, dysentery and typhoid rapidly spread throughout the camps.

This was never more true than what happened during the winter of 1777–78 at Valley Forge. It is estimated that more than two thousand Continental soldiers died from diseases.

Yellow Springs, Chester County, was named by the Lenape Indians because the springs had a yellow tint. People from Philadelphia were to learn of the healing properties of the iron spring water. Doctors began to prescribe patients trips to Yellow Springs to partake of the springs.

In the spring of 1774, Dr. Samuel Kennedy purchased Yellow Springs. After the Battle of the Brandywine, General George Washington came to the Yellow Springs Inn for a rest. He got to know the history of the healing qualities of the springs. He also got to know Dr. Kennedy.

General George Washington visited the Yellow Springs Revolutionary War Hospital several times. He came for one last visit prior to leaving Valley Forge to say goodbye to the soldiers who remained in the hospital. *Courtesy of the Alice and David Lane Collection, Historic Yellow Springs Moore Archives.*

The Yellow Springs Revolutionary War Hospital was the largest military hospital in Pennsylvania and was the only army hospital built by Congressional order during the Revolutionary War. *Courtesy of the Historical Society of Pennsylvania, Stauffer Collection.*

Seeing so many men die at Valley Forge from noncombat issues, Washington called on the Continental Congress to build a hospital to care for his soldiers. Dr. Kennedy offered to loan some of his property on which to build a hospital.

Toward the end of 1777, the various buildings and barns were used to care for the sick soldiers from Valley Forge. Realizing that these temporary facilities were not meeting the need, on January 3, 1778, Washington went before Congress and presented a plan to build a hospital to care for his men. The plan was approved, Dr. Kennedy's offer of his land was accepted and construction was begun in December 1777.

Up until this point, so-called hospitals were actually homes, barns, outbuildings and places of worship. Yellow Springs Hospital became the only hospital commissioned during the Revolutionary War. This was also the first military hospital built in North America, as well as the largest military hospital in Pennsylvania.

Dr. Bodo Otto was a German-born doctor who was the surgeon-in-chief at the Yellow Springs Hospital. The hospital became known as one of the

Ruins of the Yellow Springs Revolutionary War Hospital. *Courtesy of the Historic Yellow Springs Moore Archives.*

The Chester Springs Historical Marker highlights the Yellow Springs Revolutionary War Hospital. *Courtesy of the Pennsylvania Historical and Museum Commission.*

best-run military hospitals. On May 13, 1778, George Washington visited the hospital to check in on his men. Washington was pleased with what he saw: a well-run hospital.

Dr. Otto and his staff at the Yellow Springs Hospital cared for more than 1,300 sick men. The mortality rate was less than one out of six men, which at the time was a decent number. The hospital closed in 1781, at which time Yellow Springs reverted back to being a spa.

With the outbreak of the Civil War, the Yellow Springs Spa ceased operations. After the war, it was never able to open again, although several attempts were made. Once the Civil War ended, the Commonwealth of Pennsylvania purchased Yellow Springs and transformed the property into the Chester Springs Soldiers' Orphans School.

All that is left of Yellow Springs Hospital after two fires is the stone foundation, which visitors to Yellow Springs can view. Visitors can also enjoy the eighteenth-century Medicinal Herb Garden located there, maintained by the Philadelphia Unit Herb Society of America. Both serve as silent memorials to all who suffered and served there.

East Vincent Township: East Vincent German Reformed Church and Revolutionary War Cemetery

In East Vincent Township, there is the United Church of Christ—some call this church the "Historic Church High on the Hill." This church sits on the site of the oldest congregation in East Vincent Township, dating back to 1733. This is when settlers who had emigrated from the lower Rhine Provinces in Europe wanted to have their "divine services." Not having a meetinghouse in which to worship at the time, they met in a home of one of the settlers.

As their numbers grew, the need for a church building did as well. The first church building was a log cabin built around 1751. As was the custom, the building served as a church and a schoolhouse. Initially, the building was utilized by the German Reformed members and the Lutheran members.

As more people moved into the area, the church building became too small for both congregations. The Lutherans stayed in the original building, and the German Reformed built another log cabin about a mile from the original one in 1756. Little did these members know the supporting role they would play in the American Revolution.

September 11, 1777, witnessed the Battle of Brandywine, and some of the wounded soldiers needed a place to receive care. Furthermore, the fall and winter of 1777–78 were particularly difficult for the American Revolutionary troops, which were camped at Valley Forge. Many of the soldiers became ill with fever and needed to be cared for.

At the time, because there were no hospitals close by, the First German Reformed Church (the first church on the site of the United Church of Christ) became a place to bring these wounded and sick soldiers. Members of the church removed the pews from the church in order to convert the church into a makeshift hospital.

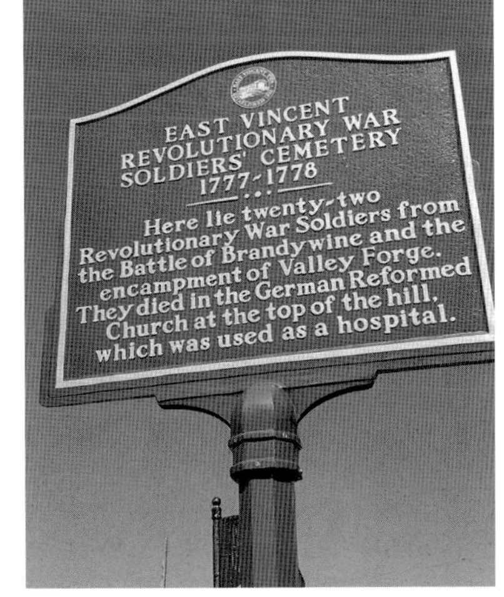

Historic marker commemorating the Revolutionary War Soldiers' Cemetery. *Author's collection.*

Although many soldiers who were cared for survived and were able to return to their homes, some did not survive. Twenty-two young soldiers died in the spring of 1778 while at the First German Reformed Church Hospital. One of the church members, Henry Hipple, donated land just down the hill and across the roadway that would become Route 23 to bury these men.

The final resting place for these twenty-two soldiers was neglected and forgotten until 1831, when the Union Battalion of Volunteers of Chester County resolved to build a memorial befitting these twenty-two heroic men.

Twenty-two Revolutionary War soldiers are buried at this cemetery. *Author's collection.*

On November 19, 1831, the foundation for the memorial was put in place, as fundraising continued in order to build a stone enclosure for the cemetery and the monument.

On October 25, 1833, the formal dedication for the monument and cemetery, known today as the Revolutionary War Soldiers' Cemetery, took place. Annual ceremonies took place beginning in 1831. Unfortunately, the annual observance stopped, and the cemetery was neglected and forgotten.

Did You Know?

First School House in West Chester, Pennsylvania

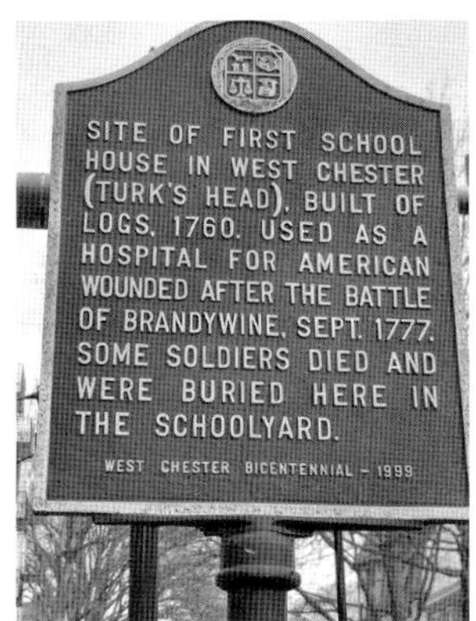

The first schoolhouse in West Chester was a log cabin built around 1760. After the Battle of the Brandywine, the school building served as a temporary hospital. *Author's collection.*

Just outside of the Iron Hill Brewery in West Chester, Pennsylvania, is a small marker that indicates the site of the first schoolhouse in West Chester. The schoolhouse was built of logs around the year 1760. During the American Revolution, an important battle was fought called the Battle of Brandywine, which took place on September 11, 1777. Wounded from that battle were taken to this schoolhouse, which was used as a temporary hospital. Some of the soldiers who died while at the schoolhouse/hospital were buried in the schoolyard.

In the early 1990s, the East Vincent Historical Commission met with the East Vincent Township and agreed to assume ownership of the property. Starting in 1994, an annual celebration honoring the twenty-two soldiers began again.

The original log cabin that housed the German Reformed Church was torn down in 1817, and a new church was built. The original church is no longer in existence, but the care the members provided for the soldiers of the American Revolution is immortalized through the cemetery just down the hill.

WEST CHESTER: FIRST BIOGRAPHY OF ABRAHAM LINCOLN

As the presidential election of 1860 was approaching, it appeared that Abraham Lincoln was being considered as a strong contender for the Republican nomination. The issue was that many people did not know who he was, and that could be a problem in the election.

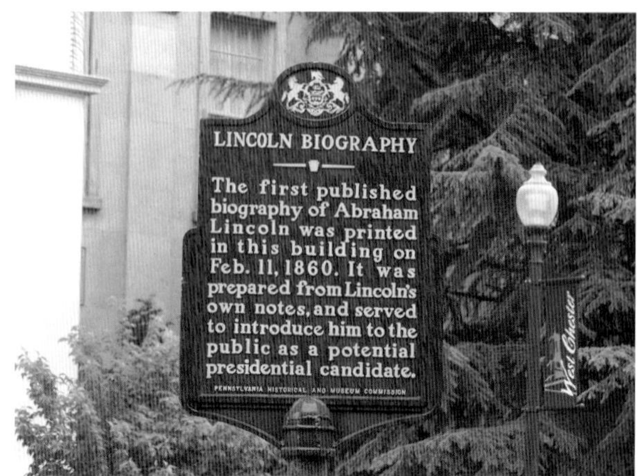

The Republican Chester County newspaper the *Chester County Times* ran the first biography of Abraham Lincoln. Republican newspapers throughout the North ran the article to introduce Lincoln to many people. It is believed that this helped him win the nomination and ultimately the presidency. *Courtesy of the Pennsylvania Historical and Museum Commission.*

Joseph Lewis was the publisher of the Republican Chester County newspaper the *Chester County Times*. Lewis believed that he could assist Lincoln with his nomination by informing as many people as possible just who Lincoln was and what he stood for. Lincoln was scheduled to go to New York City to deliver his first speech on February 27, 1860. Lewis knew that it was important to have a biography available prior to the speech in order to ensure a more positive and informed audience, which in turn could result in Lincoln clinching the Republican nomination.

Lewis rented space for his newspaper from William Everhart, who happened to be the wealthiest man in West Chester. Everhart was a staunch abolitionist who believe that it was "his sacred duty to seek the end of slavery." As it turned out, owning the building and renting out a portion to Lewis provided the opportunity to promote Abraham Lincoln, which in turn resulted in the Emancipation Proclamation. So, Everhart was able to fulfill his sacred duty not through activism or politics but rather through a commercial partnership with Lewis.

Lewis had a friend who lived in Illinois and just happened to be friends with Lincoln. Lewis reached out to Jesse Fell and asked him to request Lincoln write up an autobiographical piece. Lewis believed that he would be able to transform it into a biographical article.

Part of what Lincoln wrote was a description of himself. He stated, "I am, in height, six feet, four inches, nearly, lean in flesh, weighing, on an average, one hundred and eighty pounds; dark complexion, with coarse dark hair, and grey eyes—no other marks or brands recollected."

In the biography, Lewis noted that Lincoln "held slavery to be an institution in conflict with the principles of free government, wholly

The Lincoln Building is where the first biography of Abraham Lincoln was written and printed. *Author's collection.*

dependent upon positive law, and never to be extended where it could be legitimately prohibited."

Some people were questioning Lincoln's loyalty to the new Republican Party. Lewis put that concern to rest when he stated, "Mr. Lincoln has repeatedly given his powerful aid in support of the Republican cause in other States." After portraying Lincoln as having the temperament and wisdom to hold the office of the president of the United States, Lewis ends the biography as describing Lincoln as "an honest patriot."

Lewis completed the biography, and it was published in the *Chester County Times* on February 11, 1860, under the title of "ABRAHAM LINCOLN." Republican newspapers throughout the North reprinted the article. This turned out to be the first biography most people had ever read. Later in the year, Lewis was the person who secured the Pennsylvania delegates for Lincoln at the Republican National Convention.

In 1952, a Pennsylvania Historical Marker was placed in front of what was then known as the Everhart Building to mark where the first biography of Abraham Lincoln was written and printed. Thereafter, the building became known as the Lincoln Biography Building, or just the Lincoln Building.

The Lincoln Building was placed in the National Register of Historic Places in 1979.

UPPER OXFORD TOWNSHIP: HINSONVILLE MEN AND THE UNION ARMY

Prior to the Emancipation Proclamation, African American men could not serve as soldiers in the Union army. They could be cooks or stable hands, among other jobs. The Emancipation Proclamation opened the door to serving as Union soldiers.

President Lincoln believed that the Civil War was not a war to end slavery, but rather a war to prevent the United States from disintegrating. Abolitionists, on the other hand, believed that the reason for the Civil War was to end slavery. With that goal in mind, abolitionists also believed that African Americans should be able to fight for their freedom.

On January 1, 1863, the Emancipation Proclamation became law. That law stated, "Such persons [African American men] of suitable conditions, will be received into the armed services of the United States." Becoming a soldier could mean a pathway to citizenship. As Frederick Douglass said once, "The black man gets upon his person the brass letters, U.S.…he has earned the right to citizenship in the United States."

Eighteen Hinsonville men enlisted in the Union army:

- Samuel Henry Blake, 127th
- Charles William Cole, 24th
- James Cole, 54th Massachusetts
- Josiah Cole, 54th Massachusetts
- Amos Daws, 127th
- George W. Duffy, 22nd
- Robert G. Fitzgerald, 54th Massachusetts
- Hugh Hall, 25th
- Isaac Amos Hollingsworth, 127th
- George Jay, 54th Massachusetts
- Wesley Jay, 54th Massachusetts
- Lewis Palmer, 25th
- Stephen J. Ringgold, 22nd
- Abraham Stout, 41st
- Albert G. Walls, 54th Massachusetts

The governor of Massachusetts in 1863 was an abolitionist named John A. Andrew. At the time, there were not many African American residents in Massachusetts. However, the governor issued the Civil War's first call for African American soldiers. Within two weeks, more than one thousand Black men had volunteered. Along with the six Hinsonville men, two of Frederick Douglass's sons, Charles and Lewis Douglass, also enlisted in the 54th.

On May 28, 1863, 1,007 Black soldiers and 37 white officers marched through the streets of Boston in preparation for going off to war. Among the cheering crowds that lined the streets were William Lloyd Garrison and Frederick Douglass.

Governor John Andrew, who only a short two weeks prior had issued a call for Black soldiers, addressed the crowd and the soldiers, saying, "I know not where in all human history to any given thousand men in arms there has been committed a work at once so proud, so precious, so full of hope and glory as the work committed to you."

The parade ended, the celebration ended, the crowds left and the soldiers waited until the evening, when they boarded a ship headed to Charleston, South Carolina. The ship landed in South Carolina on June 3. Fort Wagner guarded the Port of Charleston, and that was the target for the 54th Massachusetts.

Albert Walls went missing during the Battle of Sol Legare near Charleston, South Carolina, and has always been presumed to have been killed in battle. *Author's collection.*

Colonel Robert Gould Shaw was just twenty-five years of age when he became a colonel in the 54th. Shaw was a well-known abolitionist and believed that he could promote antislavery sentiment by serving with his African American soldiers.

Colonel Shaw gathered 600 of his men, and on July 18, 1863, he led his men into battle. The battle was a disaster, and 280 of the 600 soldiers were "killed, captured, wounded, or captured." Colonel Shaw, leading the charge, was shot and killed instantly. The Battle for Fort Wagner became one of the first major conflicts fought by African American Union soldiers.

The Confederate Congress had previously announced that if any Black Union soldier were captured, he would be sold into slavery and that any captured white Union officer would be shot. Following through on that promise, all 280 Union soldiers were thrown into an unmarked grave along with Colonel Shaw.

The Confederates sent a telegram notifying the Union army that "we have buried [Shaw] with his n*****s." The Confederates hoped that this would discourage white Union army officers from further fighting with Black Union soldiers. Much to the chagrin of the Confederates, the opposite happened. When Shaw's parents were asked what they thought about what happened to their son, their response was that they could think of "no holier place" for their son to be buried than "surrounded by…brave and devoted soldiers."

Although the 54th lost the battle, its heroic actions paved the way for more recruitment of Black soldiers. In part because of the actions of the 54th, more than 180,000 African Americans joined the Union army, and they came to make up 10 percent of the Union army and navy. The 54th showed white Union officers and politicians that they could fight as well as their white counterparts. Furthermore, the 54th launched a campaign that demanded the same pay as white soldiers.

Of the eighteen men who enlisted from Hinsonville, six enlisted in the 54th Massachusetts Infantry. Albert G. Walls, Josiah Cole and James Cole were cousins. The other three who enlisted in the 54th were brothers—George, Wesley and William Jay. Of these six 54th men, five returned home. Albert Walls went missing during the Battle of Sol Legare Island, Charleston, South Carolina, and it is thought that he was killed in action.

WEST CHESTER: CIVIL WAR DRUMMER BOY

Charley Edwin King was born on April 4, 1849, to Pennell and Adaline Bennett King. Charley and his seven siblings, along with their parents, lived in West Chester, Pennsylvania. Charley loved music and especially liked to drum. The Civil War began in 1861 when Charley was only twelve years of age.

Charley believed that he was a pretty good drummer and asked his father if he could enlist in the Union army as a drummer boy. Initially, Charley's father told him no. Things changed after the Union army lost the Battle of Fort Sumter, Charleston, South Carolina. This was the first battle of the Civil War.

After this Union loss, men were asked to volunteer in the Union army for a period of three months. At this point, most people thought that this would be a short war. Many men from West Chester volunteered. A local grocer whom Charley's parents knew, Captain Benjamin Sweeney, was the leader of Company G of the 2nd Pennsylvania Infantry Regiment.

Knowing Sweeney, Charley's parents let him go with Sweeney to Harrisburg to be a part of the three-month training time. This was Charley's first experience as a drummer boy. However, during this time, Company G was ordered to the front, and Charley's parents demanded Charley come home.

Charley was not happy with this turn of events and would frequently ask him parents to let him enlist. During this time, his father would often find Charley practicing drumming in his room. Charley had gotten a taste of what it meant to be a drummer boy and wanted to return. His parents were reluctant to let him return until Captain Sweeney came to talk to them.

Sweeney and Company G took part in the Battle for Bull Run. Shortly after the three-month enlistment period was over, Sweeney came home. Believing that the war was not going to be a short affair, he formed Company F of the 49th Pennsylvania Volunteer Infantry. Sweeney had taken notice of Charley and his drumming ability during the short time he was with Sweeney in Harrisburg and wanted Charley to join him in the 49th.

Sweeney went to talk to Charley's parents and reassured them that a drummer boy was a noncombat position and that drummer boys usually were not out in front in battle. This was often the case; however, sometimes even being a distance from the main fighting did not guarantee safety.

Sweeney assured the parents that he would keep an eye on Charley and that there was little to worry about. The parents finally gave their permission, and on September 12, 1861, Charley became a member of the Union army as a drummer boy.

Drummer boys were an important part of the military. During battle, it was often hard to hear the orders being given by officers due to the noise. However, drumming was used to signal commands that could be heard by the troops. Along with the job of drumming, drummer boys also served as messenger boys and stretcher carriers.

Charley was an excellent drummer, maintained a clear and calm head during battle and was promoted quickly. Entering the 49th Pennsylvania Volunteer Infantry Regiment as a drummer boy, he soon rose to the rank of drum major.

Charley took part in the Peninsula Campaign and the Seven Days Battles. Then came the Battle of Antietam. The battle fought on September

Charley King, a drummer in the Union army, was, at age thirteen, the youngest casualty in the Civil War. *Author's collection.*

17, 1862, was to be the bloodiest battle of the Civil War. That one-day battle resulted in 22,717 dead, wounded or missing.

Charley and the 49th were not in the heaviest part of the battle. General Hancock, who was the brigade commander, came to check on the 49th and ordered it to fall back in order to be out of range. This was done. Even though the 49th had fallen back, the Confederates began to shell the men. A shell exploded, and a piece of shrapnel hit Charley, piercing his lung. He was taken to a field hospital and provided aid; however, three days later, he died—one of 2,100 Union army casualties.

Thus, Charley, at age thirteen, became the youngest Union army casualty of the Civil War. Nobody knows where Charley is buried. It could be in a mass grave located at Antietam. The parents of Charley are buried at the Green Mount Cemetery in West Chester, Pennsylvania.

A local Boy Scout by the name of Brendan Lyons heard the story of Charley King and wanted to do something to honor him. For his Eagle Scout project, Brandan raised money to have a memorial made for Charley. Brandan was able to obtain donations from the West Chester VFW along with other donations from local citizens and businesses.

Today, the Charley Edwin King Drummer Boy memorial is close to his parents' gravestones. Also buried close to Charley's parents is Charley's Civil War officer, Captain Benjamin Sweeney. Although Charley's final resting place is unknown, his drum in on display at the Antietam Battlefield Visitors' Center Museum.

Charley Edwin King represents the sacrifices many made during the Civil War. Fortunately, these sacrifices were not made in vain; instead, enslaved people would be set free, and a nation on the brink of destruction would remain intact.

WESTTOWN TOWNSHIP: CAMP ELDER

Parole camps were established during the Civil War because both the Union and Confederate armies were not prepared to house and care for prisoners of war. The rationale behind parole camps was not a humanitarian one, but rather one of logistics.

There were too many captured soldiers for either side to house and feed—or, in some cases, provide medical care for the wounded. This resulted in captured Union and Confederate soldiers being granted battlefield paroles and sent back to their respective sides to be held in a parole camp as a noncombat soldier.

An example of this would be captured Confederate soldiers being paroled. These Confederate soldiers would return to their side and promise not to return to battle until an equal number of Union soldiers had been exchanged. This was basically an honor system where the Union or Confederate side would provide housing and food for their own soldiers, and those soldiers would not return to active duty until a formal prisoner exchange took place.

How this was to be administered was developed through the Dix-Hill Cartel. Major General John A. Dix on the Union side and Major General D.H. Hill on the Confederate side met in July 1862 and created the terms. In theory, the captured soldier could be granted a battlefield parole and sent back to a parole camp to wait until an exchange had taken place, at which point he could return to combat.

However, as was often the case, the Dix-Hill Cartel was not always administered as designed. The Union army set up parole camps and held men there. The Confederate army, on the other hand, usually just sent captured soldiers home asking them to promise that they would wait until notified that an exchange had been made prior to returning to battle.

West Chester was aware that paroled Union soldiers were being sent there. In order to house the soldiers, the Horticultural Hall (now the Chester County History Center) along with private homes were used. As the numbers grew, the men were transferred to the county fairground (now West Chester University). When even more soldiers arrived, it was determined that a larger place was needed, and Camp Elder was utilized.

Camp Elder was established in July 1862 and was located in Westtown Township, Chester County. Initially, the Camp Elder site was supposed to be a training camp for the United States Colored Troops. The site had been selected by Captain James Elder.

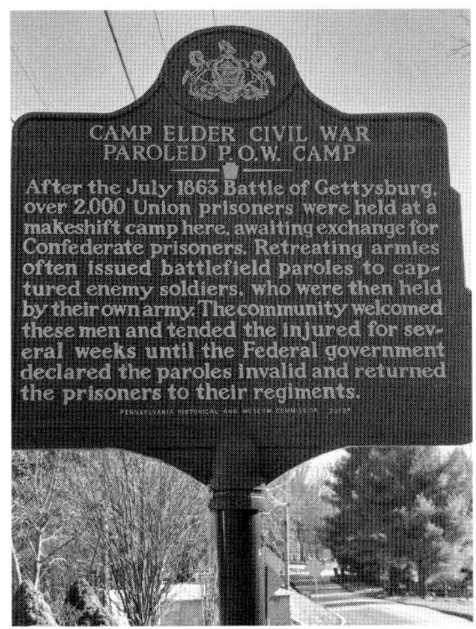

Camp Elder was a parole/POW camp established in West Chester to house Union soldiers captured by the Confederate army. *Courtesy of the Pennsylvania Historical and Museum Commission.*

The recruitment of African Americans was not producing the numbers hoped for. In addition, there was a large number of paroled Union army soldiers from the Battle of Gettysburg. This resulted in Camp Elder being designated a parole camp—officially known as Camp Elder Civil War Paroled Prisoner of War Camp.

More than two thousand Union paroled soldiers were sent to Camp Elder. At this point, it was farmland owned by Enoch William. Barracks had to be built and food found. Local citizens, in the meantime, opened up their homes for the soldiers. Militia from Philadelphia and Delaware County were sent to Camp Elder to guard the paroled soldiers.

During this time, the paroled soldiers were allowed to work in nearby farmers' fields and even visit their relatives with the promise to return in the evening. Many of the paroled soldiers had been wounded during the Battle of Gettysburg, and quite a few died while at Camp Elder. Many of those who perished were buried at nearby Green Mount Cemetery.

Camp Elder was in operation from mid-July until August 1863. It was at this time that the federal government decided that the Confederate battlefield paroles issued to the Camp Elder Union soldiers were null and void and that the soldiers were released, resulting in many men returning to active duty.

In September 2013, the Pennsylvania Historical and Museum Commission, along with the Brandywine Valley Civil War Roundtable, held a dedication service for the Camp Elder Historic Marker.

KENNETT SQUARE BOROUGH: CAMP BLOOMFIELD

When you think of the War of 1812, what comes to mind? Perhaps Washington, D.C., which the British burned in 1814. Or maybe Baltimore, Maryland, or even Philadelphia, Pennsylvania—all potential British targets. But Kennett Square, Pennsylvania?

The War of 1812 was a war in the making for a number of years. For many years, the British Royal Navy impressment of men was considered a valid form of recruitment. Up until this time, the concept of national sovereignty per international maritime law only applied to a nation's navy, which meant non-military vessels were open to impressment. This practice may have worked in the past, but it did not sit well with the young country of the United States of America. More than six thousand U.S. citizens had been taken by the Royal Navy.

This practice by the Royal Navy is considered to be one of the factors that led President James Madison to sign the paperwork on June 18 that formally began the War of 1812. James Madison was known to quote Benjamin Franklin, who had stated, "The War of Revolution is won, but the War for Independence is yet to be fought."

On August 26, 1814, people in Philadelphia heard about the burning of Washington, D.C. Many believed that Philadelphia might be the next target of the British. Militia were called up for duty, and Brigadier General Joseph Bloomfield was the commander of the Fourth Military District, Philadelphia.

A call was put forth by Pennsylvania governor Simon Snyder for militia to muster in the counties surrounding Philadelphia. Many answered the call, including Benjamin Gratz of Philadelphia. He was a second lieutenant in the Washington Guards. He and his unit went to Camp Bloomfield near Kennett Square.

At the time, the village of Kennett Square consisted of "eight dwellings, five of which were log cabins making it one of the largest villages in the area." Located on what is now the Anson B. Nixon Park was Camp Bloomfield, named after Brigadier General Joseph Bloomfield. There were about three thousand men located there under the command of the brigadier general.

Another concerned citizen who volunteered his service was a young man by the name of William Thackara, also of Philadelphia. On September 1, 1814, he joined the Third Company of the Washington Guards. While with the Washington Guards, he served at Camp Bloomfield.

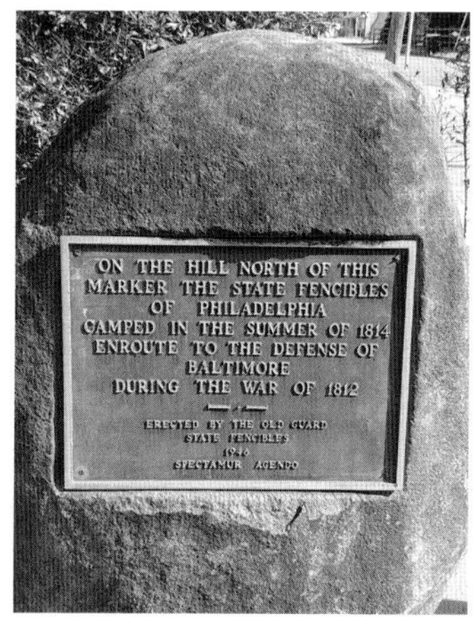

The War of 1812 resulted in Kennett Square being the host for Brigadier General Joseph Bloomfield and three thousand of his men. *Author's collection.*

In one of his letters to his father while stationed at Camp Bloomfield, young Thackara wrote that the "business and duties of a camp constant and fatiguing, a solder's life not a lazy one. Camp pleasantly situated. Country round delightful. People of Kennett in general hospitable."

If you are traveling out of Kennett Square on the way to Longwood Gardens, you will see the store the Country Butcher. Just prior to that, sitting on an island in the middle of the road, is a boulder on which is attached a plaque marking the War of 1812 Camp Bloomfield.

The War of 1812 resulted in Kennett Square being host to Brigadier General Bloomfield and three thousand of his men. The war also called on a young company by the name of DuPont to produce much of the gunpowder for the troops. Then there was the attack on Fort McHenry, which resulted in a young man by the name of Francis Scott Key writing the words that would become the United States of America's national anthem.

CHESTER COUNTY: CHESTER COUNTY WAR AID ASSOCIATION

On April 6, 1917, the United States of America declared war on the German empire. This was almost three years since the war began. Many men and women from Chester County served in the war.

Realizing that there was a need for assistance, the Chester County War Aid Association (CCWAA) was organized in December 1917. CCWAA was a relief organization designed to help the soldiers and nurses who were overseas fighting the war.

The CCWAA held drives to collect various items that those serving overseas would benefit from. According to the Chester County Archives' article "Chester County War Aid Association," CCWAA provided such items as "sweaters, socks, combs, and Christmas package, comfort bags, tobacco, helmets, mirrors, and local newspapers."

Along with the clothes and related item drives, the CCWAA hired local companies to knit sweaters. Other knit items were made by local women, who were happy to provide a touch of home for the men and women. There were times when the wrong item was sent to a soldier. One time, a soldier stationed in a desert area received a sweater. He sent it back asking that it be sent to a soldier, where it would be appreciated.

These items meant a lot to the men and women. One Chester County man, Christie Collopy, wrote to the CCWAA on August 14, 1918, to thank

The Chester County War Aid Association was organized in 1917 to help the soldiers and nurses who were overseas fighting in the war. The CCWAA also provided clothes for those displaced from the war. *Courtesy of the Chester County History Center.*

the association for sending a local newspaper: "Things are pretty hard at the present time over here. So when a letter or paper comes it makes you forget the fighting for a while."

Another vital service the CCWAA provided was assisting veterans returning from the war find gainful employment. Isabel Darlington was the secretary for CCWAA, and she sent each returning Chester County veteran a letter of welcome, which included asking the veteran if he needed assistance finding a job.

Ms. Pierre S. duPont donated the funds necessary to set up a "Reconstruction Center" at Longwood on May 12, 1919. This center consisted of forty-eight beds to serve the needs of the sick or wounded soldiers, and it continued to do so until 1921.

Another important service the CCWAA provided was keeping records of all the Chester County soldiers and nurses who served during World War I. Soldiers and nurses were listed as missing in action, killed in action or returned home.

The CCWAA archival collection includes "cards, correspondence, an account book of items sent to soldiers and nurses overseas, and miscellaneous

WWI reference materials and clippings collected by Secretary Isabel Darlington," according to the Chester County Archives. These items are stored at the Chester County Archives, 601 Westtown Road, Suite 080, West Chester, Pennsylvania, 19380 (ccarchives@chesco.org). Hours are Monday to Friday, 9:00 a.m. to 4:00 p.m.

PHOENIXVILLE: VALLEY FORGE MILITARY GENERAL HOSPITAL

Construction on the Valley Forge General Hospital (VFGH) to treat the wounded of World War II was authorized by the Office of Chief of Engineers in Washington, D.C., on April 1, 1942. Actual construction on the VFGH began in May 1942, and it opened on February 22, 1943.

The hospital was built on 182 acres of farmland located in Charlestown Township, Chester County. There were more than one hundred buildings on the property, and the hospital had a capacity for more than 3,000 patients. There were 1,600 staff, including officers, nurses, enlisted men and WACS. The hospital had "eight operating rooms, mobile x-ray units for bedfast patients, five complete dental offices, and complete chemical and biological laboratories," according to Galloway Morris's "A History of Valley Forge General Hospital."

At the time it opened, it was the largest military hospital in the United States. Eventually, it became the second-largest hospital on the East Coast, with Walter Reed being larger. By 1944, VFGH became known throughout the world for its work "in the field of plastic surgery and eye surgery, and in the rehabilitation of the war blinded." Patients blinded in battle were brought to VFGH as quickly as possible in order to receive treatment. A holistic treatment approach was utilized in order to assist the patient learn to mentally cope with being blind, as well as physically to adapt to this new way of life.

During World War II, VFGH also housed German and Italian POWs.

Besides treating wounded soldiers, VFGH was a teaching hospital. In the late 1960s, a "Clinical Specialist" course was offered. This was a ten-month training program that was the equivalent of a LPN. In January 1962, VFGH offered a six-month psychiatric nursing training course for Army Nurse Corps officers. In 1972, VFGH offered a twenty-one-week-long Occupational Therapy Specialist course.

During the Korean War and the Vietnam War, many of the wounded were treated at VFGH. Between January 1, 1968, and September 30,

Left: When Valley Forge General Hospital opened in 1943, it was the largest military hospital in the United States. It is the only military general hospital named after a place instead of a military/medical-military person. *Courtesy of the Pennsylvania Historical and Museum Commission.*

Right: In 1974, the Valley Forge General Hospital closed. In 1976, the Valley Forge Christian College took over the property. As the school expanded, it became the University of Valley Forge. *Author's collection.*

1970, VFGH cared for more than seven thousand soldiers wounded in the Vietnam War.

On April 17, 1973, the closing of VFGH was announced by the hospital commander, Colonel Phillip Deffer. In his remarks, he stated:

> *Valley Forge General Hospital, over the past 31 years, has faced many challenges of great complexity, and it has met each head on, has succeeded and has walked away proud that it accomplished that mission. It's now my duty to officially inform you of the next challenge facing us. At this hour in Washington, the Secretary of Defense is having a public news conference, at which he is announcing the entire base realignment package…Valley Forge will be closed.* [VFGH officially closed in 1974.]

There were sixty-five military general hospitals in the United States. All but one—Valley Forge General Hospital—was named for a military person or a medical-military person. By doing so, the history of Valley Forge and all that took place there was forever honored.

The Vietnam War was winding down, and by 1974, VFGH closed. In 1976, the Valley Forge Christian College took over the closed VFGH. As the college expanded, it became the University of Valley Forge.

WEST CHESTER: PENICILLIN

On April 28, 2023, the Chester Country History Center held the world premiere of the documentary *The Mushroom Man Who Changed the World: G. Raymond Rettew*. This documentary was produced by Deborah Divine (the granddaughter of G. Raymond Rettew) and Doug Gahm.

This section of the book was being written prior to the documentary being released. The author believes that this is an important part of Chester County history, and for those not familiar with this topic, he wanted to introduce the reader to G. Raymond Rettew and his lifesaving work.

Rettew was born and raised in West Chester, Pennsylvania. One of his summer jobs was working at the Strode Pork Products factory, where he got to know Joseph W. Strode, who owned the company. Upon high school graduation, Rettew studied chemistry at the University of Delaware and Swarthmore College.

After completing college, Rettew obtained employment at the Hires Company in Philadelphia. Calling on his chemistry training, Rettew said, "One of the best things I did for Hires was the introduction of pH control. This was new, and much was not in the textbooks. It was necessary to build a pH meter and make my own set of conversion tables," according to Mark Dixon's "The Mushroom Man."

Southern Chester County was home to many mushroom farms, so it was no surprise that Rettew's father-in-law owned one. Rettew often heard his father-in-law talk about the lack of a consistent quality mushroom spawn, which is needed to grow mushrooms.

Having solved one chemistry-related issue at Hires, Rettew wondered if his background in chemistry could help solve the issue of the lack of quality mushroom spawn. Having maintained his friendship with his old boss, Joseph Strode, he shared his father-in-law's dilemma.

Shortly thereafter, Strode, who had the funds, and Rettew, who had the chemistry background, began the Chester County Mushroom Laboratories (CCML) in West Chester. Being a chemist, Rettew developed a system that utilized sterile growing conditions, which resulted in a high-quality mushroom spawn.

As Rettew further studied mushrooms, he came across the work of Alexander Fleming and his accidental discovery of penicillin in 1928. While doing research on bacteria, Fleming noticed a mold in one of his petri dishes of bacteria that killed the bacteria. This turned out to be *Penicillium notatum*; what Fleming called "mold juice" had oozed from the mold.

Dr. Desmond Biel and G. Raymond Rettew with penicillin culture. *Courtesy of the Chester County History Center.*

Rettew learned about Alexander Fleming and the "mold juice," as well as the research by two Oxford (England) scientists, Howard Florey and Ernst Chain, which showed the dramatic effects penicillin had on bacterial infections.

With the outbreak of World War II, Raymond learned that oftentimes soldiers did not die from their wounds but rather from the infections that resulted from the wounds. There appeared to be a need for large amounts of penicillin to combat bacterial infections. Being so familiar with mushroom spawn and growing mushrooms, Raymond wondered if he could use similar techniques to grow penicillin.

Rettew used his equipment at CCML to grow penicillin. The results were outstanding, and a large amount of penicillin was able to be produced; however, the penicillin produced quickly broke down. Rettew came up with a rather simple solution: he employed a cream separator that milk producers used to separate the cream from the milk. By using the separator, Rettew was able to separate the pure penicillin from the growth medium.

Remarkably, by mid-1943, this little West Chester company, CCML, was the major producer of penicillin in the United States, with the majority of it being sent to the military. Rettew stated that "as a result of this program in 1943, the first penicillin was produced commercially. We produced more penicillin than the total of all other manufacturers in the world."

Needing a larger facility, Walnut Street Laboratories was built. With this larger space, by the fall of 1943 the Walnut Street Laboratories had become the world's major penicillin producer.

In 1945, Alexander Fleming (later Sir Alexander Fleming visited G. Raymond Rettew at his laboratory to tour the facility. During an interview, Fleming stated, "It isn't exaggerating to say that G. Raymond Rettew beat the whole world at the work of producing penicillin in more than laboratory quantities. Countless men wounded on European battlefields are alive today who would have died save for the first shipments made here under his directions and rushed overseas."

Southern Chester County is well known for growing mushrooms, but many did not realize that it was also the first major producer of penicillin,

G. Raymond Rettew, Sir Alexander Fleming and Alfred Barol, technical director of John Wyeth and Brother Inc. *Courtesy of the Chester County History Center.*

G. Raymond Rettew and his company, Chester County Mushroom Laboratories, became the major producer of penicillin in the United States. *Courtesy of the Pennsylvania Historical and Museum Commission.*

which resulted in countless numbers of World War II men being saved. Prior to penicillin being used in World War II, many soldiers died from the infections that resulted from their wounds. G. Raymond Rettew was able to change that.

Sir Alexander Fleming summed up the work of G. Raymond Rettew when he said, "There are wounded men living today who would have died had it not been for the pioneer work of G. Raymond Rettew, of West Chester, in the field of penicillin."

BIBLIOGRAPHY

Adams, Charles J. "A Day Away: Serpentine Rock Makes Nottingham a Special Place." *Reading Eagle*, July 14, 2016. Accessed October 13, 2022. https://www.readingeagle.com/2016/07/14/a-day-away-serpentine-rock-makes-nottingham-a-special-place.

Adrienne, Carole. "A Memorial for a Teenage Soldier: Charles Edwin 'Charlie" King." *Civil War X*, 2015. Accessed March 22, 2023. https://www.civilwarx.blogspot.com/2015/05/a-memorial-for-teenage-soldier-charles.html.

Allis, B. "Mr. Griffen's Gun." *News from Phoenix Steel Corporation*. Housed at Phoenixville Historical Society under "Phoenix Iron Company—Griffen Gun 1982–1989; 1989.16.32.c."

American Chemical Society. "Discovery and Development of Penicillin." Accessed May 3, 2023. https://www.acs.org/education/whatischemistry/landmarks/flemingpenicillin.html.

Association for the Colonial Theatre. "Blobfest 10." Summer 2009. Housed at Chester County History Center under "Phoenixville Business Houses—Colonial Theatre."

Azzollini, Mike, and Robert Azzollini. "The 1876 Centennial Monorail." PWEB, March 4, 1999. Accessed October 24, 2022. https://www.pweb.netcom.com/-gemmalou/1876.html.

Barber, Edwin A. "Examination of Indian Graves in Chester County, Pennsylvania." *American Naturalist* 13, no. 5 (1879): 294–99. Accessed March 3, 2023. https://www.jstor.org/stable/2449459.

Bastas, Dimitros N. *Etruscan Majolica: The Majolica of Griffen, Smith & Company*. Vol. 1, *The History*. New York: AO Books, 2009.

Bastin, Edson S. *Feldspar Deposits in the United States*. Washington, D.C.: U.S. Geological Survey/Department of the Interior, 1910.

Berlin, Ira. *Generations of Captivity: A History of African-American Slaves.* Cambridge, MA: Belknap Press of Harvard University Press, 2003.

Bertram, Mike. "The Bottling Plant at Colonial Springs." *Tredyffrin Easttown History Quarterly* 47, no. 3 (2010): 84–87.

———. "Tredyffrin in 1710." *Tredyffrin Easttown Historical Society History Quarterly* 47, no. 4 (2020): 108–10.

Blanco, Richard L. "American Army Hospitals in Pennsylvania during the Revolutionary War." *Pennsylvania History: A Journal of Mid-Atlantic Studies* 48, no. 4 (1981): 347–68.

Blockson, Charles L. *Hippocrene Guide to the Underground Railroad.* New York: Hippocrene Books Inc., 1994.

Borough of Downingtown. "History of the Log House." Accessed October 9, 2022. https://www.downingtown.org/historic-commission/pages/history-log-house.

Brennen, Neil. "Revolutionary War Cemetery, East Vincent, Chester County, PA, July 4, 2014." A Taste for the Woods, July 4, 2014. Accessed November 28, 2022. https://atasteforthewoods.com/?=1309.

Brody, Susannah *Remembering Chester County Stories from Valley Forge to Coatesville.* Charleston, SC: The History Press, 2010.

Bruno, Frank. "Valley Forge Army Hospital: 30 Years of Military Medical Care." National Museum of Health and Medicine, May 14, 2021. Accessed January 17, 2023. https://medicalmuseum.health.mil.micrograph/index.cfm/posts/2021/Valley-forge-army-hospital.

Calarco, Tom. *People of the Underground Railroad: A Biographical Dictionary.* Westport, CT: Greenwood Press, 2008.

Chadds Ford Historical Society. "Family, Women, and Children and Gender Roles in the Lenape Tribe." July 22, 2016. Accessed March 6, 2023. https://chaddsfordhistorical.wordpress.com/2016/07/22/family-women-and-children-and-gender-roles-in-the-lenape-tribe.

———. "Leni Lenape: Dreams, the Art of Healing and Death and Burial Practices." July 28, 2016. Accessed March 9, 2023. https://chaddsfordhistoricl.wordpress.com/2016/07/28/lenni-lenape-dreams-the-art-of-healing-and-death-burial-practices.

Chambless, John. "The Downingtown Log House: More than 300 Years and Counting." *Chester County Press*, September 9, 2017. Accessed October 9, 2022. https://www.chestercounty.com/2017/09/07/154286/the-downingtown-log-house-more-than-300-years-and-counting.

———. "Remembering the Fun of Years Gone By—Lenape Park." *Chester County Press*, April 1, 2019. Accessed October 15, 2022. https://www.chestercounty.com/2019/04/01/193666/rememberring-the-fun-of-years-gone-by.

Chemical Elements. "Chromium." 2023. Accessed March 12, 2023. https://thechemicalelements.com/chromium.

Cheney, Jim. "Hiking the Mount Misery Trails to the Abandoned Colonial Springs Bottling Plant at Valley Forge." Uncovering Pennsylvania. Accessed April 6, 2023. https://uncoveringpa.com/mount-misery-trails-valley-forge.

———. "Hiking Through the Beautifully Unique Nottingham Serpentine Barrens of Nottingham County Park." Uncovering Pennsylvania, November 9, 2021. Accessed November 4, 2022. https://www.uncoveringpa.com/hiking-nottingham-serpentine-barrens.

Cherran, Nathan. "10 Interesting Facts about Chromium." Infomory, 2015. Accessed March 13, 2023. https://infomory.com/facts/10-interesting-facts-about-chromium.

Chester County. "History of the Chester County Poorhouse." Accessed November 2, 2022. https://www.chesco.org/1791/History-of-the-Chester-County-Poorhouse.

———. "Nottingham County Park Serpentine Barrens National Natural Landmark Heritage Hike." Accessed September 29, 2022. https://www.chesco.org/DocumentCenter/View/26864/Heritage-Hike-Final?bidid=.

———. "Nottingham Park." Accessed November 4, 2022. https://www.chesco.org/nottingham-park-chester-county-PA.

Chester County & Preservation. "History of Nottingham Park Serpentine Barrens." Accessed December 29, 2022. https://www.chesco.org/4698/history.

Chester County Archives. "The Chester County War Aid Association." February 27, 2019. Accessed January 18, 2023. https://www.chesco.org/Blog.aspx?IID=4.

———. "County War Aid Association (WWI), 1917–1921." Accessed January 13, 2023. https://chesco.org/1706/County-War-Aid-Association-WWI-1917-1921.

Chester County Conference and Visitors Bureau. "Nottingham County Park." Accessed December 31, 2022. https://www.brandywinevalley.com/location-details/nottingham county park.

Chester County Historical Society with the Chester County Camera Club. *Then and Now Chester County*. Charleston, SC: Arcadia Publishing, 2004.

Chester Heights Neighborhood Alliance. "Lenape Park." June 21, 2019. Accessed October 24, 2022. https://www.facebook.com/CHNeighborsAlliance/posts/throwback-thursday-postlenape-parksome-of-you-may-remember-lenape-park-a-local-a/46159.

Chrome History. "Discovery of Chrome in Year 1839 Was Cause for Excitement." *Jeffersonian*, February 2, 1859. Housed at Oxford Area Historical Association under "Chromite Mining" folder.

"Chromite Deposits in Serpentine, MD., PA., DE." Housed at Oxford Area Historical Association under "Barrens—History" folder.

"Chromite Deposits in Serpentine, MD., PA., DE." Part 2. Housed at Oxford Area Historical Association under "Barrens—History" folder.

Cope, Thomas D. "The Stargazers' Stone." *Pennsylvania History: A Journal of Mid-Atlantic Studies* 4, no. 6 (1939): 205–20. Accessed October 23, 2022. https://www.jstor.org/stable/27766373.

Daily Local News. "From Our Archives: When Frederick Douglass Held His Last Speech at West Chester." April 6, 2017, updated August 19, 2021. Accessed September 23, 2022. https://www.dailylocal.com/2017/04/06/from-our-archives-whjen-frederick-douglass-held-his-last-speech-at-west-chester.

———. "Living History: Small Town Has Big Influence on America." January 18, 2013, updated August 19, 2021. Accessed November 2, 2022. https://www.dailylocal.com/2013/01/18/living-history-small-town-has-big-influence-on-America.

Dean, Eddie. "O Brother, Where Art the Sunsets of Yesteryear?" Bluegrass West, October 31, 2001. Accessed October 12, 2022. https://www.bluegrasswewst.com/ideas/sunsetpark.html.

Dean, Nora Thompson. "Some of the Ways of the Delaware Indian Women." Delaware Tribe, August 7, 2016. Accessed March 5, 2023. https://delawaretribe.org/blog/2016/08/07/some-of-he-ways-of-the-delaware-indian-women.

Deeban, John P. "Impressment of Seaman Charles Davis by the U.S. Navy." *National Archives* 44, no. 2 (Summer 2012): 1–10.

Delaware County Community College Archives. "Alumni of the Former Downingtown Industrial and Agricultural School Will Join College Officials September 30 to Celebrate the Rich Legacy of the Former School for African Americans." September 28, 2021. Accessed December 5, 2022. https://www.dccc.edu/news/09292021/alumni-former-downingtown-industrial-and-agricultural-school-will-join-delaware-county.

Delaware County Times. "Longwood Progressive Meetinghouse and Cemetery Honored by National Park Service." January 20, 2015. Accessed September 29, 2022. https://www.delcotimes.com/news/longwood-progressive-meetinghouse-and-cemetery-honored-by-the-national-park-service/article_aa5e28b4-01b7-569b-80ce-9724c6ed30e.html.

Densmore, Christopher. "Truth for Authority, Not Authority for Truth." Kennett Underground Railroad Center, May 22, 2005. Accessed October 21, 2022. https://www.kennettundergroundrr.org/truth-for-authority-not-authority-for-truth.

Dixon, Mark E. "Charley King's Civil War Drum Career." Mainline Today, August 16, 2013. Accessed December 29, 2022. https://mainlinetoday.com/life-style/main-line-history-charley-kings-civil-war-drum-career.

———. "The Mushroom Man." Mainline Today, February 23, 2011. Accessed May 1, 2023. https://mainlinetoday.com/life-style/the-mushroom-man/amp.

———. "Reexamining the Story Behind Indian Hannah." Pennsylvania Historic Preservation, December 13, 2017. Accessed March 5, 2023. https://pahistoricpreservation.com/remembering-indian-hannah.

———. "The Story of Westtown's Little-Known Civil War Camp." Mainline Today, February 27, 2020. Accessed December 5, 2022. https://mainlinetoday.com/life-style/the-story-of-westtowns-little-known-civil-war-camp.

Donehoo, George P. "The Indians of the Past and the Present." *Pennsylvania Magazine of History and Biography* 46, no. 3 (1922): 177–198. Accessed March 4, 2023. https://www.jstor.org/stable/20086480.

Dorchester, Jane Elizabeth. "The Evolution of Serpentine Stone as a Building Material in Southeastern Pennsylvania: 1727–1931." Master's thesis, University of Pennsylvania, Philadelphia, 2001.

Dowling, Iris G., ed. *History of Churches & Worship Groups in the Oxford Area*. Oxford, PA: Oxford Area Historical Association, 2012.

Duff, Susie, and John Duff. "A Bark in the Park—Nottingham Park." Hike With Your Dog. Accessed March 15, 2023. https://hikewithyourdog.com/a-bark-in-the-park-philadelphia.

Dugan, Mary L., and Ella J. Sestrich. *East Linden Street: A History—Abolition, Industry & Diversity in Kennett Square, PA*. Kennett Square, PA: Kennett Underground Railroad Center, 2008.

East Brandywine Township. "Bondsville Mill—Historic Resource Report." Accessed December 17, 2022. https://www.ebrandywine.org/DocumentCenter/View/460.

East Brandywine Township/Bondsville Mill Park Committee. "History of Bondsville Mill." Accessed December 17, 2022. https://www.ebrandywine.org/286/Bondsville-Mill-Park-Committee.

———. "History of the Mill Site." Accessed December 5, 2022. https://www.bondsvillemillpark.org/history.html.

East Coventry Township. "East Coventry Township History—Schuylkill Canal." Accessed September 27, 2022. https://www.eastcoventry-pa.gov/index.asp?SEC=87D45CA3-C1BB-494F-A1C9-89B6C86B1BDF&Type=B_Basic.

———. "East Vincent Church of Christ—Part 2." Accessed January 15, 2023. https://www.eastvincenjt.org/index.asp.

———. "Revolutionary War Monument—East Vincent, PA." Accessed November 28, 2022. https://www.eastvincent.org/index.asp?SEC=C56936DC-9F52-418D-BCF3-234F0F069DD5.

Ecenbarger, William. *Walkin' the Line*. New York: M. Evans and Company Inc., 2000.

Elhassan, Khalid. "Fascinating Civil War Facts that Won't Be in the History Books." History Collection, February 8, 2021. Accessed December 19, 2022. https://historycollection.com/fascinating-civil-war-facts-that-won't-be-in-the-history-books/18.

Esch, Jim. "Where Life's Foundations Are Carved in Stone—Chester County's Captivating Green Stone." Housed at Oxford Area Historical Association under "Barrens—History 6008.002" folder.

Evening Bulletin. "First Monorail Was Made in Phoenixville." September 1, 1976. Photo housed at Phoenixville Historical Society under "Phoenix Iron Company—Commercial Products—1982–1991."

Ewing, Agnew R., MD. *The West Grove Community Hospital*. West Grove, PA: self-published, 1959.

ExplorePAhistory. "Chester Springs Historical Marker." Accessed October 17, 2022. https://www.explorepahistory.com/hmarker.php?markerld=1-A-D3.

———. "G. Raymond Rettew Historical Marker." Accessed September 23, 2022. https://www.explorepahistory.com/hmarker.php?markerld=1-A-2F2.

———. "Great Minquas Path Historical Marker." Accessed September 27, 2022. https://explorepahistory.com/hmarker.php?markerld+1-A-209.

———. "Indian Hannah (1730–1802) Historical Marker." Accessed January 6, 2023. https://explorepahistory/hmarker.php?markerld=1-a-226.

———. "Lincoln Biography Historical Marker." Accessed September 19, 2022. https://www.explorepahistory.com/hmarker.php?markerId=1-A-11c.

———. "Minguannan Indian Town Historical Marker." Accessed January 5, 2023. https://explorepahistory.com/hmarker.php?markerId=1-A-12c.

———. "Phoenix Iron Company Historical Marker." Accessed February 20, 2023. https://explorehistory.com/hmarker.php?markerId=1-A-2BD#.

Fisher, George R., MD. "Serpentine Rock from Serpentine Barrens." Philadelphia Reflections, June 29, 2010. Accessed December 29, 2022. https://www.philadelphia-reflections.com/blog/1834.html.

Foner, Eric. *Gateway to Freedom: The Hidden History of the Underground Railroad*. New York: W.W. Norton & Company Inc., 2015.

Freese, Kerry S. "Built Beneath a Darkening Cloud." April 4, 1990. Housed at the Oxford Area Historical Association under "Railroads/Peachy—6198.009."

Friedman, Don. *Improvements in Design: Analysis, Design, Steel, and Wrought Iron.* New York: Old Structures, 2021.

Friends of the Oxford Public Library. *Around the Oak—Oxford, Pennsylvania.* Oxford, PA: Hubley's Offset Printing, 1999.

Friends of White Clay Creek Preserve. "Historic Resources—London Tract Meeting House and Cemetery." Accessed March 6, 2023. https://friendsofpawcop-org.doodlekit.com/home/historic-resources.

Fry, Herb "The Amusement Park on the Trolley Line." *Tredyffrin Easttown History Quarterly* 30, no. 3 (1992): 87–100.

Galle, Karen. "Camp Elder Civil War Paroled POW Camp." Pennsylvania Heritage, Spring 2014. Accessed December 22, 2022. https://paheritage.wpengine.com/article/camp-elder-civil-war-paroled-pow-camp.

Gaw, Richard. "Penn Township Dedicates Historical Marker in Tribute to Sunset Park." *Chester County Press*, August 14, 2018. Accessed September 27, 2022. https://www.chestercounty.com/2018/08/14/178522/penn-township-dedicates-historical-marker-in-tribute-to-sunset-park.

Gentzel, John. "Phoenixville Guns Helped Determine Civil War Outcome." Housed at Phoenixville Historical Society under "Phoenix Iron Company—Griffen Gun 2000-2008; 2022.36.8."

Geocaching. "KSQ and the War of 1812." Accessed April 29, 2023. https://www.geocaching.com/geocache/GC3XW56_ksq-and-the-war-of-1812.

Golovin, Anne Castrodale. "William Wood Thackara, Volunteer in the War of 1812." *Pennsylvania Magazine of History and Biography* 91, no. 3 (1967): 313–25.

Gooch, Cheryl Renee. *Hinsonville's Heroes: Black Civil War Soldiers of Chester County, Pennsylvania*. Charleston, SC: The History Press, 2018.

———. *On Africa's Lands: The Forgotten Stories of Two Lincoln Educated Missionaries in Liberia*. Lincoln University, PA: Lincoln University Press, 2014.

Handout for the Phoenixville Armed Forces Day May 11, 1963 Celebration. Housed at Phoenixville Historical Society under "Phoenix Iron Company—Griffen Gun 2000-2008; 2008.28.4."

Hansen, Brett. "History Lesson: Orchestrating the Obelisk: The Washington Monument." 2008. Accessed February 19, 2023. https://ascelibrary.org/doi/pdf/10.1061/ciegag.0000812.

Harper, Douglas. "The Barren Ridges of W. Nottingham: Held a Fortune for Some Lucky People." *Daily Local News*. Housed at Oxford Area Historical Association under "Barrens History."

Harper, Douglas R. *West Chester to 1865: That Elegant & Notorious Place*. West Chester, PA: Chester County Historical Society, 1999.

Harvey, Frederick L. *The History of the Washington National Monument and Washington National Monument Society*. Washington, D.C.: Government Printing Office, 1903.

Hazlett, James C., Edwin Olmstead and M. Hume Parks. *Field Artillery Weapons of the Civil War*. Newark: University of Delaware Press, 1988.

Heathcote, C.W., Sr. *A History of Chester County, Pennsylvania*. Harrisburg, PA: National Historical Association Inc., 1932.

Herb Society of America-Philadelphia Unit. "History of Historic Yellow Springs." Accessed January 9, 2023. https://www.hsapphiladelphia.org/history-of-yellow-springs.

Historical Marker Database. "Camp Elder Civil War Paroled P.O.W. Camp." Accessed December 17, 2022. https://www.hmdb.org/m.asp?m=68586.

———. "Minguannan Indian Town." Accessed January 5, 2023. https://www.hmdb.org/m.asp?m=168374.

Historical Society of Phoenixville. "Valley Forge General Hospital Marker." Accessed January 15, 2023. https://www.hspa-pa.org/Valley-forge-general-hospital-marker.html.

History. "The 54th Massachusetts Infantry." April 14, 2010. Accessed October 25, 2022. https://www.history.com/topics/american-civil-war/the-54th-massachusetts-infantry.

Hoffman, Steven. "Racing to Protect Historic Treasures in the White Clay Creek Preserve." *Chester County Press*, July 5, 2022. Accessed March 6, 2023. https://www.chestercounty.com/2022/07/05/405104/racing-to-protect-historic-treasures-in-the-white-clay-creek-preserve.

Holland, Brenna O'Rourke. "Schuylkill Navigation Company." Philadelphia Encyclopedia, 2015. Accessed December 23, 2022. https://www.philadelphiaencyclopedia.org/essays/schuylkill-navigation-company.

Homan, Wayne E. "Griffen Designs a Cannon." *Philadelphia Magazine* (October 17, 1965). Housed at Phoenixville Historical Society under "Phoenix Iron Company—Griffen Gun 1991–1999; 1997.912.1."

Hoopes, Joshua. "West Chester Boarding School for Boys." May 23, 1837. Housed at Chester County History Center under "West Chester Private Schools."

Hoppe, Jonathan. "Where Chester County Buried It's Poor and Forgotten." May 12, 2020. Accessed October 3, 2022. https://www.hoppejl.wordpress.com/2020/05/12/where-chester-county-buried-its-poor-and-forgotten.

Houting, Scott P. "The 3-Inch Ordnance Rifle Developed by John Griffen Became the Civil War's Most Reliable Fieldpiece." *America's Civil War* (January 2022): 14, 72 and 74.

Hudson, Chad. "White Clay Creek Pennsylvania Park and Preserve." Storymaps, September 15, 2019. Accessed March 6, 2013. https://storymaps.arogis.com/stories/5a94fa6cad20466abe042fdc9d6e0323.

Hunt Magazine. "Chester County's Poorhouse" (Fall 2015). Accessed November 4, 2022. https://www.thehuntmagazine.com/feature/chester-countys-poorhouse.

Jacobson, Eric. "Chromium: A Thoroughly Modern Metal." Accessed March 4, 2023. https://sites.dartmouth.edyu/toxmetal/more-metals/chromium-a-thoroughly-modern-metal.

James, Arthur E. *A Brief History of the Geology and Mineralogy of Chester County*. New York: Lewis Historical Publishing Company Inc., 1943.

———. *The Potters and Potteries of Chester County, Pennsylvania*. Exton, PA: Schiffer Publishing Limited, 1978.

Jeffers, H. Paul. "Mr. Griffen's Gun: How a New Method of Forging a Cannon Gave the Union a Superb Fieldpiece." *Civil War Times* 3, no. 7 (1961): 9–10.

Johnson, Johnny. "The Nottingham Serpentine Barrens and Wood Mine—Some Historical Notes." *Friends of Mineralogy Pennsylvania Newsletter* 31, no. 1 (2003).

Johnstone, Malcolm. *For the Union*. West Chester, PA: Chester County Community Foundation, 2020.

Jones, James. "A Brief History of Transportation in West Chester." Digital Commons, 2001. Accessed March 4, 2023. https://digitalcommons.wcupa.edu/hist_wchest/70.

Jorgensen, C. Peter "Development of the Three-Inch Ordnance Rifle; Drawing Found." *Muzzle Loading Artilleryman* 3, no. 3 (1982): 6–16.

Justice Bell Foundation. "The Justice Bell Story." Accessed September 23, 2022. https://www.justicebell.org/the-justice-bell-story.

Kashatus, William C. *Just Over the Line: Chester County and the Underground Railroad*. West Chester, PA: Chester County Historical Society, 2002.

Kashatus, William C., and Anthony J. Stavenski, eds. *Traveling the Eastern Line: Student Essays on Southeastern Pennsylvania's Underground Railroad*. West Chester, PA: Star Printing Inc., 2002.

Kegerise, Cory, and Karen Galle. "Remembering Indian Hannah." Pennsylvania Historic Preservation, May 28, 2014. Accessed January 6, 2023. https://pahistoricpreservation.com/remembering-indian-hanna.

Kelly, Maeve. "The 1852 Pennsylvania Women's Rights Convention." CC Women and Girls, March 29, 2017. Accessed September 28, 2022. https://www.ccwomenandgirls.org/the-1852-pennsylvania-womens.

Kennett Township, Pennsylvania. "History of Kennett Township." Accessed October 5, 2022. https://www.kennett.pa.us/2118/History-of-Kennett-Township. https://www.kennett.pa.us/218/History-of-Kennett-Township.

———. "War of 1812." Accessed April 28, 2023. https://www.kennett.pa.us/218/History-of-Kennett-Township.

Kiddle: Kids Encyclopedia Facts. "Downingtown Industrial and Agricultural School Facts for Kids." Accessed December 19, 2022. https://kids.kiddle.co/Downingtown_Industrial_and_Agricultural_School.

King of Prussia Historical Society. "Justice Bell History and Celebratory Events." August 13, 2013. Accessed October 13, 2022. https://www.kophistory.org/justice-bell-history-and-celebratory-events.

Kline, Benjamin F.G., Jr. *Little, Old, and Slow: The Life and Trials of the Peach Bottom and Lancaster, Oxford, and Southern Railroads*. Lancaster, PA: Benjamin F.G. Kline Jr., Publisher, 1985.

Knickerbocker, Ken. "Did You Know? How the Brandywine River Got Its Name." December 4, 2018. Accessed January 5, 2023. https://vista.today/2016/12/how-the-brandywine-river-got-its-name.

Knoff, E.B., and J.V. Lewis. *Chrome Ores of Southeastern Pennsylvania and Maryland*. Washington, D.C.: United States Geological Survey/Department of Interior, 1922.

Kummer, Frank. "A Native American Burial Ground in Chester County Is Returning to Its 'Rightful Owners.'" *Philadelphia Inquirer*, April 13, 2022. Accessed January 9, 2023. https://www.inquirer.com/news/lenape-burial-ground-chester-county-pennsylvania-delaware-nation-20220413.html.

Landefeld, William R., Jr. *The Changing Boundaries of Pennsylvania from 1493–1921*. Kinzers, PA: Davco Advertising Inc., 2009.

Lang, Patricia. "A Tour of the London Tract Meeting House." *Newark Post*, June 7, 2007. Accessed March 6, 2023. https://www.newarkpostonline.com/features/a tour of the london tract-meeting-house/article.

Lanyon, Mark. *Abolition and the Underground Railroad in Chester County, Pennsylvania*. Charleston, SC: The History Press, 2022.

Lefko, Andy. "The Life of Charlie King." Bradbury Camp #149. Accessed March 22, 2023. https://www.bradbury149.org/bc-ar-king01.htm.

———. "The Youngest Casualty: The Life of Charlie King." Civil War X, December 14, 2018. Accessed December 19, 2022. https://civlwarrx.blogspot.com/2015/03/the-youngest-casualty-life-of-charlie.html.

Licht, Walter, Mark Frazier Lloyd, J.M. Duffin and Mary D. McConaghy. "The Original People and Their Land: The Lenape, Pre-History to the 18th Century." Collaborative History. Accessed March 3, 2023. https://collaborativehistory.gse.upenn.edu/stories/original-people-and-their-land-lenape-pre-history-18th-century.

Lincoln University. "Lincoln University Partners with American Experience to Populate the Abolitionist Map of America." December 3, 2012. Accessed October 28, 2022. https://www.lincoln.edu/news-and-events/news/lincoln-university-partners-american-experience-populate-abolitionist-map.

Linda Hall Library Resources. "Standardization of American Rail Gauge." Accessed April 13, 2023. https://railroad.lindahall.org/essays/rails-gauge.

Lininger, Jay L. "The Poorhouse Quarry: Revisiting a Classic Location." *Friends of Mineralogy Pennsylvania Newsletter* 31, no. 1 (2003).

Locust Grove Schoolhouse. "Indian History." Accessed January 6, 2023. https://locustgroveschoolhouse.org/articles/indian-history.

———. "Lenape Park." Accessed October 25, 2022. https://www.locustgroveschoolhouse.org/articles/lenape-park.

Longwood Progressive Friends Meetinghouse. *Bulletin for the 150th Anniversary Celebration*. Sunday, May 22, 2005, Kennett Square, Pennsylvania. Housed at the Chester County History Center under box "Society of Friends, Meetings L-M," West Chester, Pennsylvania.

Lookingbill, Todd R., PhD, et al. *Evaluation of the Nottingham Park Serpentine Barrens, Chester County, Pennsylvania*. Frostburg: University of Maryland Press, 2007.

Lower Merion Historical Society. "The Lenape." Accessed March 3, 2023. https://lowermerionhistory.org/?page_id=186902.

Lucas, Loraine. "Abraham Lincoln's Quaker Roots Traced to the Barnards of Chester County and the Kennett Underground Railroad." *Chester County Day* 76, no. 1 (2016): 14–15. Accessed November 16, 2022. https://www.marlboroughmeeting.org/V2/Abraham%20Lincoln%20Quaker%20Roots%20to%20Barnards%20of%20CC%209-2016.pdf.

Lukens, Rob. "County Contributed to World's Chrome Supply." *Daily Local News*, September 26, 2004. Housed at Oxford Area Historical Association under "Barrens History—6011.003" folder.

Lukens, Rob, and Sandra S. Momyer. *Yellow Springs*. Images of America series. Charleston, SC: Arcadia Publishing, 2007.

Lutz, Walter J. "Diamond Rock School." *Tredyffrin Easttown Historical Society History Quarterly* 18, no. 1 (1980): 3–14.

Majolica Society. "Etruscan Majolica (Griffen, Smith, and Hill)." Accessed October 27, 2022. https://www.majolicasociety.com/griffen-smith-hill.

Mammana, Zachary, and Pamela Curtin. "Woman's Rights Convention of 1852 Historical Marker." The Clio, May 9, 2020. Accessed September 28, 2022. https://www.theclio.com/entry/100145.

Mason, Alden J. "Aboriginal Archeological Sites in Chester County." *Tredyffrin Easttown Historical Society Quarterly* 3, no. 1 (1940): 2–12. Accessed March 3, 2023.

McFeely, Tim. "Lancaster, Oxford and Southern." Railroad History Explorer, August 6, 2013. Accessed December 18, 2022. https://rrexplorer.wordpress.com/2013/08/06/lancaster-oxford-and-southern-2.

McGee, D.F. *The Peach Bottom Railway Company*. Lancaster, PA: Lancaster County Historical Society, 1923.

McIntyre, Ken, and Ken Weaver. "Roselyn Theater." Cinema Treasures. Accessed October 5, 2022. https://www.cinematreasures.org/theaters/23325.

Mikulich, Leah. "Chester County History Center to Present 'The Mushroom Man Who Changed the World.'" *Montco Today*, March 29, 2023.

Momyer, Sandy. *The History of Historic Yellow Springs*. Chester Springs, PA: Historic Yellow Springs Inc., 2021.

———. "Yellow Springs." *Tredyffrin Easttown Historical Society History Quarterly* 27, no. 3 (1989): 83–92.

Moore, Carl Gordon, Jr. "Okehocking Indian Town." Historical Marker Database, December 14, 2011. Accessed September 27, 2022. https://www.hmdb.org/m.asp?m=159371.

———. "On the Site of This Veterans Memorial." Historical Marker Database, June 19, 2021. Accessed October 3, 2022. https://www.hmdb.org/m.asp?m+182325.

Moore, J. Arthur. "Charles 'Charley' King." 2020. Accessed March 15, 2023. https://www.arthurmore.com/category/uncategorized.

Morris, Galloway. "A History of Valley Forge General Hospital." Schuylkill Township. Accessed January 5, 2023. https://www.schuylkilltwp.org/wp-content/uploads/HistoryArticles/1-The-Valley-Forge-General-Hospital.pdf.

Mullin, Paul. "The Original People—The Lenni Lenape." *Westtown Gazette* 23 (Fall 2017): 4–5.

Naik, Suraj. "The Unbreakable Bond Between a Town and a Gelatinous Monster." Accessed December 16, 2022. https://pabook.libraries.psu.edu/literary-cultural-heritage-map-pa/feature-articles/unbreakable-bond-between-town-and-gelatinous.

Nathan, Roger E. *East of the Mason-Dixon Line: A History of the Delaware Boundaries.* Dover: Delaware Heritage Press, 2000.

Nielson, Euell A. "Hosanna African American Union Methodist Protestant Church (1843–)." Black Past, November 2, 2015. Accessed November 24, 2022. https://www.blackpast.org/african-american-history/hosanna-african-american-union-methodist-protestant-church-1843.

Norris, John V. "Griffen Gun Was Even at Battle of Gettysburg." *Daily Republican,* May 16, 1963. Housed at Phoenixville Historical Society under "Phoenix Iron Company—Griffen Gun 1991–1999; 1994.73.1."

Olszewski, George J. *A History of the Washington Monument, 1844–1968, Washington, DC.* Washington, D.C.: Office of History and Historic Architecture, 1971.

Oxford Library. "Oxford Library: Oldest Library of Record in Chester County." *Discover Oxford* (November 1997). Housed at Oxford Area Historical Association under "Oxford—Odds and Ends."

———. Write-up about the Oxford Library. Housed at Oxford Area Historical Association under "Oxford—Odds and Ends—6198.054, Drawer 20."

Park, Katie. "A Chester County Village Was Vacated for a Nuclear Power Plant. Today, It's a Ghost Town." *Philadelphia Inquirer,* August 3, 2018. Accessed September 15, 2022. https://www.inquirer.com/philly/news/pennsylvania/fricks-locks-village-ghost-town-excelon-limerick-east-coventry-20180803.html.

Parks, W.G., et al. *Statement of Scope, Condition, Purposes and Needs of Downingtown Industrial School, 1907–1908.* Philadelphia, PA: Banner Publishing Company, 1907.

Pearre, Nancy C., and Allen V. Heyl Jr. *Chromite and Other Mineral Deposits in Serpentine Rocks of the Piedmont Upland Maryland, Pennsylvania and Delaware.* Washington, D.C.: U.S. Geological Survey/Department of the Interior, 1960.

———. *The History of Chromite Mining in Pennsylvania and Maryland.* Harrisburg, PA: U.S. Geological Survey: 1959.

Pennsylvania Department of Conservation and Natural Resources. "History of White Clay Creek Preserve." Accessed March 3, 2023. https://www.dcnr.pa.gov/stateparks/findapark/whiteclaycreekpreserve/pages/history.aspx.

Pfingsen, Bill. "Lincoln Biography—Placed on the National Register of Historic Places—1979." Historical Marker Database, June 5, 2008. Accessed September 7, 2022. https://www.hmdb.org/m.asp?m=184093.

Philadelphia Magazine. "This Lesser-Known Liberty Bell Played a Big Role in Pa. Women's Suffrage" (June 24, 2019). Accessed September 23, 2022. https://www.phillymag.com/news/2019/06/24/justice-bell-womens-suffrage.

Philadelphia Tribune. "Alumni Celebrate Legacy of School for African Americans." October 5, 2021. Accessed December 18, 2022. https://www.phillytrib.com/metros/delaware_county/alumni-celebrate-legacy-of-school-for-african-americans/article_5d4fa9d0-6e4d-5de7-a0a3-da1d8ada811d.html.

Photo of the Prismoidal Railway. Housed at Phoenixville Historical Society under "Phoenix Iron Company—Commercial Products 1992.2007; 2003.43.1."

Pinkowski, Edward. *Chester County Place Names*. Philadelphia, PA: Sunshine Press, 1962.

Pirro, J.F. "Etruscan Majolica Pottery's Historical Phoenixville Ties." Mainline Today, January 18, 2012. Accessed October 27, 2022. https://mainlinetoday.com/life-style/etruscan-majolica-potterys-historical-phoenixville-ties.

Pisasale, Gene. "Living History: Markers to a Forgotten War." *Unionville Times*, February 28, 2013. Accessed April 17, 2023. https://www.unionvilletimes.com/?p=14152.

PocketSights. "East Linden Street, Kennett Square, Pennsylvania, 19348." Accessed December 29, 2022. https://pocketsights.com/tours/place/East-Linden-Street-35539.

———. "Kennett Area Underground Railroad Self-Guided Driving Tour." Accessed November 17, 2022. https://pocketsights.com/tour/Kennett-Square-The-Underground-Railroad-Story-in-Kennett-Square-Chester-County-PA-1355.

———. "Longwood Progressive Friends Meetinghouse and Cemetery c. 1855." Accessed November 13, 2022. https://pocketsights.com/tours/place/Longwood-Progressive-Friends-Meetinghouse-and-Cemetery-c-1855.

Price, Robert W. "The Historic Church High on the Hill—Part 1." East Vincent United Church of Christ. Accessed April 11, 2023. https://www.eastvincent.org/index.asp?SEC=8F56DD09-3E6D-48AF-ADE4--27E1B0CC4484.

Quillman, Catherine. "History Matters—Lenape Park." 2003. Accessed April 14, 2023. https://catherinequillman.com/history-matters.

Rellahan, Michael P. "A Visit to Chester County's Burial Site for Forgotten Souls." *Daily Local News*, March 3, 2012. Accessed January 12, 2023. https://www.dailylocal.com/2012/03/03/a-visit-to-chester-countys-burial-site-for-forgotten-souls.

Rettew, Bill. "Sunset Park Recognized with Historical Marker." *Daily Local News*, August 14, 2018/updated August 19, 2021. Accessed September 9, 2022. https://www.dailylocal.com/2018/08/14/sunset-park-recognized-with-historical-marker-amp.

Roberts, Gail. "The Oxford Caramel Company." *Oxfordian* 48 (Spring/Summer 2022): 62–67.

———. "Oxford Train Station." *Oxfordian* 44 (Spring/Summer 2020): 47–50.

———. "The Wheeler Circus." *Oxfordian* 49 (Fall/Winter 2022): 62–67.

Russo, Marianne H., and Paul A. Russo. *Hinsonville, a Community at the Crossroads: The Story of a Nineteenth Century African American Village*. Selinsgrove, PA: Susquehanna University Press, 2005.

SAH Archipedia. "Historic Yellow Springs." Accessed January 18, 2023. https://sah-archipedia.org/buildings/PA-02-CH33.

Schalata, Tom, Jr. "Griffen Gun Turned Tide in War." *The Phoenix*. Housed at Phoenixville Historical Society under "Phoenix Iron Company—Griffen Gun 1991–1999; 1999.350.1."

Shultz, Elizabeth. "Hosanna Church: The Last Building in Hinsonville." Pennsylvania Historic Preservation, March 26, 2014. Accessed November 18, 2022. https://pahistoricpreservation.com/hosanna-church-last-building-hinsonville.

Simpson, Linda. "Lenape Ceremonies Burial Ceremonies of the Lenape Tribe." OKGenWeb, 2017. Accessed March 9, 2023. https://okgenweb.net/-itdelaware/ceremonies.htm.

Sklaroff, Susan. "Joseph Gratz, the First Troop and the War of 1812." March 15, 2023. Accessed April 18, 2023. https://rebeccagratz.blogspot.com/2012/02/joseph-gratz-first-troop-and-war-of-1812.

Sloto, Ronald A. *The Mines and Minerals of Chester County, Pennsylvania*. Scotts Valley, CA: On-Demand Publishing, LLC—DBA CreateSpace Independent Publishing, 2009.

Smedley, R.C. *History of the Underground Railroad in Chester and Neighboring Counties in Pennsylvania (1883)*. Mechanicsburg, PA: Stackpole Books, 2005.

Smith, Keith S. "Site of the First Schoolhouse in West Chester, Pennsylvania—c. 1760." Historical Marker Database, January 12, 2016. Accessed October 3, 2022. https://www.hmdb.org/m.asp?m=92184.

Smith, Robert C., and John H. Barnes. *Geology of Nottingham, County Park*. Harrisburg: Commonwealth of Pennsylvania Department of Conservation and Natural Resources, Bureau of Topographic and Geologic Survey, 1998.

Solutions to History. "Hospitals and Burial Grounds during the Philadelphia Campaign." Accessed January 15, 2023. https://solutionstohistory.com/post-1-revolutionary-war-hospitals-and-buirial-grounds--during-the-philadelphia-campaign.

Southern Chester County Charm. "The Serpentine Barrens Rare and Local." February 1992. Housed at Oxford Area Historical Association under "Oxford History—6014.002" folder.

Stumpes, Jax. "Historic Yellow Springs." November 14, 2020. Accessed September 9, 2022. https://jaxstumpes.blogspot.com/2020/11/historic-yellow-springs-pa-11142020.html?m=1.

Swain, Craig. "Good News Productions 1952–1974." Historical Marker Database, August 23, 2010. Accessed October 25, 2022. https://www.hmdb.org/m.asp?m=35964.

Switala, William J. *Underground Railroad in Pennsylvania*. 2nd ed. Mechanicsburg, PA: Stackpole Books, 2008.

Taylor, Francis C. *The Trackless Trail*. Kennett Square, PA: KNA Publishing, 1976.

———. *The Trackless Trail Leads On: An Exploration of Conductors and Their Stations*. West Chester, PA: Graphics Standard, 1995.

Thompson, Richard. "Sunset Park Designated a Pennsylvania Landmark." Bluegrass Today, April 25, 2018. Accessed October 25, 2022. https://www.bluegrasstoday.com/sunset-park-designated-a-pennsylvania-landmark.

Torres, Louis. *The United States Army Corps of Engineering and the Construction of the Washington Monument.* Washington, D.C.: Government Printing Office, 1984.

U.S. National Park Service. "Did You Know: The Justice Bell and the Fight for Women's Access to the Vote." Accessed September 23, 2022. https://www.nps.gov/articles/dyk-justice-bell.htm.

———. "54th Massachusetts Regiment." Accessed February 21, 2023. https://www.nps.gov/articles/54th-Massachusetts-regiment.htm.

———. "National Natural Landmarks—Nottingham Park Serpentine Barrens." 2022. Accessed March 10, 2023. https://www.nps.gov/subjects/nnlandmarks.

———. "Nottingham Park Serpentine Barrens." Accessed December 23, 2022. https://nps.gov/subjects/nnlandmarks/site.htm?Site=NOPA-PA.

University of Delaware. "Background of New London Academy." Accessed October 27, 2022. https://udel.edu/-mm/newLondon/history.html.

Upper Oxford Township & Historical Commission Newsletter. "About Our Area: What Is 'Serpentine Rock?'" (Fall 2015). Housed at Oxford Area Historical Association under "Barrens—History" folder.

Uzelac, Coni Porter. "African Americans in Chester County." Accessed September 23, 2022. https://files.usgwarchives.net/pa/chester/church/hosanna/txt.

Vircsik, Mike. "The Eight Phoenix Column Shafts Inside the Washington Monument." November 15, 2000. Housed at Phoenixville Historical Society under "Phoenix Iron Company—Commercial Products 1992–2007; 2000.724.4."

Virscik, Mike, and Steve Lorenzetti. Transcript of phone call on July 5, 2000, about the Phoenix Columns in the Washington Monument, Washington, D.C. Housed at Phoenixville Historical Society under "Phoenix Iron Company—Commercial Products 1992–2007; 2000.356.1."

Wagontown Fire Company. "89th Annual Old Fiddlers Picnic." August 13, 2017. Accessed October 24, 2022. https://wagontownfire.com/apps/public/newsView.cfm?News_ID=687.

Wallace, Paul A. *Indian Paths of Pennsylvania*. Harrisburg: Pennsylvania Historical and Museum Commission, 1965.

Walton, Peter. "54th Massachusetts Infantry Regiment (1863–1865)." Black Past, December 15, 2007. Accessed November 17, 2022. https://www.blackpast.org/african-american-history/fifty-fourth-massachusetts-infantry-1863-1865.

Weclerly, Dan. "Newly Unveiled Historical Marker in Downingtown Honors Legacy of Former School for African Americans." Vista Today, October

13, 2021. Accessed December 9, 2022. https://vista.today/2021/10/downingtown-industrial-agricultural-school.

West Chester University. "Frederick Douglass Biography." Accessed April 21, 2023. https://www.wcupa.edu/_academics/Fdouglass/biography.

West Nottingham Township. "Comprehensive Plan Draft—A Brief History of West Nottingham." Living Places, 2005. Accessed March 3, 2023. https://www.livingplaces.com/PA/Chester_County/West_Nottingham_Township.html.

Wheeler, William. "Circus Owner Alson F. Wheeler." Circus and Sideshows, 2013. Accessed November 1, 2022. https://www.circussandsideshows.com/owners/alsonwheeler.html.

Wikipedia. "Colonial Theatre (Phoenixville, Pennsylvania)." Accessed September 27, 2022. https://en.wikipedia/wiki/Colonial_Theatre_(Phoenixville,_Pennsylvania).

———. "Downingtown Industrial and Agricultural School." Accessed December 21, 2022. https://en.wikipedia.org/wiki/Downingtown_Industrial_and_Agricultural_School.

———. "Downingtown Log House." Accessed October 9, 2022. https://en.wikipedia.org/wiki/Downingtown_Log_House.

———. "Fricks Locks Historic District." Accessed September 27, 2022. https://en.wikipedia.org/wiki/Fricks_Locks_Historic_District.

———. "Great Minquas Path." Accessed September 27, 2022. https://en.wikipedia.org/wiki/Great_Minquas_Path.

———. "Hannah Freeman." Accessed March 4, 2023. https://en.wikipedia.org/wiki/Hannah_Freeman.

———. "Hinsonville." Accessed October 28, 2022. https://en.wikipedia.org/wiki/Hinsonville.

———. "History of Silk." Accessed April 7, 2023. https://en.wikipedia.org/wiki/History_of_Silk.

———. "Joseph J. Lewis." Accessed January 9, 2023. https://en.wikipedia.org/wiki/Joseph-J.-Lewis.

———. "Justice Bell (Valley Forge)." Accessed September 23, 2022. https://en.wikipedia.org/wiki/Justice_Bell_ (Valley_Forge).

———. "Lancaster, Oxford and Southern Railway." Accessed December 21, 2022. https://www.wkiwand.com/en/Lancaster_Oxford_and_Southern_Railway.

———. "Narrow-Gauge Railway." Accessed December 21, 2022. https://www.wikiwand.com/en/Narrow_gauge_railways.

———. "New London Academy (Pennsylvania)." Accessed October 24, 2022. https://en.wikipedia.org/wiki/New_London_Academy_(Pennsylvania).

———. "Okehocking Historic District." Accessed January 5, 2023. https://en.wikipedia.org/wiki/Okehocking_Historic_District.

———. "Okehocking People." Accessed March 3, 2023. https://en.wikipedia/wiki/Okehocking_people.

———. "Parole Camp." Accessed April 28, 2023. https://en.wikipedia.org/wiki/Parole_camp.

———. "Pennsylvania Woman's Convention at West Chester in 1852." Accessed December 17, 2022. https://en.wikipedia.org/wiki/Pennsylvania_Woman%27s_Convention_at_West_Chester_in_1852.

———. "Phoenix Iron Works (Phoenixville, Pennsylvania)." Accessed February 20, 2023. https://en.wikipedia.org/wiki/Phoenix_Iron_Works_(Phoenixville, Pennsylvania).

———. "Schuylkill Canal." Accessed December 23, 2022. https://en.wikipedia.org/wiki/Schuylkill_Canal.

———. "United States in World War I." Accessed May 1, 2023. https://en.wikipedia.org/wiki/United-States-in-World-War-I.

———. "Valley Forge General Hospital." Accessed January 9, 2023. https://en.wikipedia.org/wiki/Valley-Forge-General-Hospital.

———. "Washington Monument." Accessed April 4, 2023. https://en.wikipedia.org/wiki/Washington_Monument.

———. "West Chester Boarding School for Boys." Accessed March 8, 2023.

———. "White Clay Creek Preserve." Accessed March 6, 2023. https://en.m.wikipedia.org/White_Clay_Preserve.

Wilby, Ted, and Howard B. Haas. "Colonial Theatre." Cinema Treasures. Accessed October 24, 2022. https://www.cinematreasure.org/theaters/3769.

Wiley, Samuel T. *Biographical and Portrait Cyclopedia of Chester County, Pennsylvania, Comprising a Historical Sketch of the County*. Edited by Winfield Scott Garner. Philadelphia, PA: Gresham Publishing Company, 1893.

Willauer, Dave. "East Vincent Honors Revolutionary Soldiers." Spring-Ford Area Historical Society, July 7, 2021. Accessed November 28, 2022. https://www.sfahs.com/post/east-vencent-honors-revolutionary-soldiers.

Willistown Township. "Native American History—Okehocking Preserve." Accessed January 5, 2023. https://www.willistown.pa.us/DocumentCenter/View/739.

———. "Ockehocking Preserve Named after Native Americans." February 10, 2017. Accessed October 15, 2022. https://www.willistown.pa.us/facilities/facility/details/Okehocking-Preserve-6.

Wintermantel, Mike. "Valley Forge General Hospital." Historical Marker Database, January 19, 2014. Accessed October 21, 2022. https://www.hmdb.org/m.asp?m=71355.

Yarnall, Howard E. "Longwood Meeting." *Bulletin of Friends Historical Association* 17, no. 2 (1928): 49–54. Accessed October 15, 2022. https://jstor.org/stable/41943767.

Yeager, Brigid. "Unusual Ecosystem Based on Serpentine." *Daily Local News*, April 26, 1998. Housed at Oxford Area Historical Association under "Barrens History" folder.

Zimmerman, Matthew A. "Trails (Indian)." Accessed January 19, 2023. https://philadelphiaencyclopedia.org/essays/trails-indian.

Newspapers

The following newspaper articles referenced were clipped from the original newspapers and mounted on cardboard. There are no page numbers.

HOUSED AT CHESTER COUNTY HISTORY CENTER UNDER "COLONIAL THEATRE."

Daily Local News (West Chester, PA). August 22, 1929.

———. June 21, 1929.

———. March 24, 1929.

HOUSED AT CHESTER COUNTY HISTORY CENTER UNDER "INDIANS"

Daily Local News (West Chester, PA). March 23, 1950.

HOUSED AT CHESTER COUNTY HISTORY CENTER UNDER "INDIANS—LENNI LENAPE"

Daily Local News (West Chester, PA). October 7, 1990.

HOUSED AT CHESTER COUNTY HISTORY CENTER UNDER "NEW LONDON TOWNSHIP—PRIVATE SCHOOLS"

Village Record (West Chester, PA). April 23, 1886.

HOUSED AT CHESTER COUNTY HISTORY CENTER UNDER "RETTEW, WYETH LABS, AND PENICILLIN"

Daily Local News (West Chester, PA). August 14, 1945.

———. January 15, 1972.

. June 5, 1945.

Philadelphia (PA) Evening Bulletin. September 3, 1943.

Philadelphia (PA) Inquirer. August 5, 1945.

HOUSED AT CHESTER COUNTY HISTORY CENTER UNDER "TREDYFFRRIN TOWNSHIP—PUBLIC SCHOOLS"

Diamond Rock School

Daily Local News (West Chester, PA). 1926.

———. November 18, 1922.

Daily Republican (Monongahela, PA). June 26, 1964.

Philadelphia (PA) Ledger. May 20, 1931.

Philadelphia (PA) Sunday Bulletin. September 24, 1961.

Upper Main Line News (Wayne, PA). January 11, 1941.

HOUSED AT CHESTER COUNTY HISTORY CENTER UNDER "WEST CHESTER BUSINESS HOUSES—LINCOLN BIOGRAPHY"

Daily Republican (Monongahela, PA). April 24, 1937.

———. July 4, 1937.

———. June 14, 1938.

———. March 18, 1958.

———. March 15, 1957.

———. March 1, 1958.
———. March 26, 1949.
Daily Local (West Chester, PA). February 4, 1908.
———. February 8, 1908.
———. July 25, 1991.
———. June 2, 1996.
———. May 29, 1986.
Philadelphia (PA) Inquirer. March 15, 2017.

Housed at Chester County History Center under "West Chester—Private Schools"—West Chester Boarding School for Boys
Village Record (West Chester, PA). July 12, 1837.

Housed at Chester County History Center under "West Grove Business Houses—Roselyn Theatre."
Daily Local News (West Chester, PA). October 15, 1915.
———. September 16, 1915.
———. September 20, 1980.
Kennett News and Advertiser (Kennett Square, PA). November 19, 1943.
West Grove (PA) Independent. April 17, 1947.
———. January 8, 1936.

Housed at Chester County History Center under "West Pikeland Township—Private Schools"
Soldiers Orphans School
Jeffersonian (Jeffersontown, KY). April 18, 1868.
———. August 8, 1870.
Village Record (West Chester, PA). November 19, 1864.

Housed at Oxford Area Historical Association under "Automobiles Made in Oxford 2141."
Daily Local News (West Chester, PA). November 13, 1972.

Housed at Oxford Area Historical Association under "Peters Papers."
Oxford (PA) Press. April 24, 1913.
———. January 29, 1948.
———. March 9, 1892.
———. May 30, 1895.
———. May 23, 1895.
———. November 18, 1891.

Miscellaneous

Display at Oxford Area Historical Association
"1892: Business Is Booming." Covers Flowers, Oxford Milling Company, Oxford Caramel Factory and Butter Shipments.

Display at Oxford Area Historical Association
"Oxford Caramel Factory."

Housed at the Chester County History Center
Estelle Cremers Papers. "Navigation" (Early History of Schuylkill Canal). Folder 4, Box 35.

Housed at the Chester County History Center
Estelle Cremers Papers. "Navigation" (The Old Schuylkill Canal). Folder 2, Box 35.

News Release. "Isaac Tyson, Jr. Inducted into Mining Hall of Fame, Has Ties to Chester County." October 10, 1996. Housed at Oxford Area Historical Association under "Chromite Mining 2070."

ABOUT THE AUTHOR

Two Lincoln University graduates: the author (class of 1998) and the current president of Lincoln University, Dr. Brenda Allen (class of 1981). *Author's collection.*

Mark Lanyon's twenty-plus career in behavioral health was launched when he was studying for his Master of Human Services degree at Lincoln University (LU, '98). During his career, Mark supervised and/or directed numerous behavioral health programs in settings such as the prison system, probation and parole system, hospitals and inpatient and outpatient behavioral health treatment programs. Since retiring, Mark has been able to focus on research about Chester County. His research resulted in his book *Abolition and the Underground Railroad in Chester County, Pennsylvania*. This book covered slavery, the Underground Railroad, the abolitionist movement, the Pennsylvania Yearly Meeting of Progressive Friends (also known as the Longwood Progressive Friends Meeting), Hosanna Church and the founding of Lincoln University. Further research has resulted in his latest book, *Lost Chester County, Pennsylvania*, which explores the unknown, little-known and forgotten history of Chester County. Mark and his wife, Beth, live in West Grove, Pennsylvania. They have two daughters and three grandchildren. Mark is available for speaking engagements to present on both of these books. You can contact him to discuss times and dates by contacting the Marketing Department at The History Press at marketing@arcadiapublishing.com.